Click & Easy

For Teddy, the Australian Shepherd
for whom the "every dog" in this book is named.

Click & Easy
Clicker Training for Dogs

Miriam Fields-Babineau

Photos by Evan Cohen

Library of Congress Cataloging-in-Publication Data:
Fields-Babineau, Miriam.
Click & easy : clicker training for dogs / Miriam Fields-Babineau ; photos by Evan Cohen.
   p. cm.
   ISBN-13: 978-0-7645-9643-8 (pbk.)
   ISBN-10: 0-7645-9643-8
 1. Dogs—Training.   2. Clicker training (Animal training)   I. Title.
   SF431.F53   2006
   636.7'0887—dc22   2005023684
   CIP

Printed in the United States of America

10 9 8 7 6 5 4 3

Book design by Marie Kristine Parial-Leonardo, Elizabeth Brooks
Cover design by Jeff Morrow
Book production by Wiley Publishing, Inc. Composition Services

Contents

Acknowledgments

I want to thank all those who have helped in bringing this book to press, including my first line editor, Joan Macaluso, a longtime friend who was a client and is Teddy's companion; my wonderful editor at Howell Book House, Beth Adelman, who has given me encouragement and, from time to time, put the fire under my rear end to keep me going; my acquisitions editor, Pam Mourouzis, for taking a chance on me; my photographer, Evan Cohen, who keeps getting better and better at putting my thoughts and writing into a spectacular visual format; and my great dogs and companions, Peaches and Princess, who are constantly teaching me how to be a better trainer.

Introduction

I once trained dogs using coercion and force. This is the method I first learned when I became a trainer. Barbara Woodhouse was the *big thing* in the early 1980s. Her *Walkies* method, with her special jingling choke chain, was very popular with both dog trainers and owners. I used the choke chain for the correcting sound it made, and my voice to guide and communicate.

As I gained experience and new tools became available, I gradually changed my dog training approach. In the early '90s head halters gained popularity. A wonderful trainer introduced me to the tool and its appropriate use. I loved the concept of teaching the dog in a way he understands; however, this method was still a means of coercion because I used it to make the dog do what I wished. Yes, I still used my voice and visual cues to communicate in much the same way as when I used a choke chain. Because dogs need time to get used to a head halter, I used food to lure and teach before using the head halter as a tool to reinforce lessons.

Dogs are social animals and wish only to remain within their social environment. Dogs will do what they must to conform to that environment—their social pack. Hence, when they are forced to work through pain or fear, or even when they are lured with food, they respond. The response may not be, "Hey, I'm happy to work for you. Any time!" Yet they still perform, more out of fear of the consequences than the pure desire to work.

The theory behind clicker training has been around since the early part of the nineteenth century. It was introduced by several behavioral researchers who sought to understand the learning process. They asked, Do we learn best through imitation or association? Do we remember better with reinforcement or with punishment?

Overall, the outcome of all the research was the development of operant conditioning (any procedure in which a behavior is made stronger or weaker by its consequences) as a tool to train any animal of any temperament, wild or domestic. Clicker training is one method that implements the principles of operant conditioning, using positive rewards to reinforce desired behaviors.

Most dog trainers want to learn the science behind a training approach in order to fully understand it. This is a very necessary education, as we must transfer our knowledge to others. There are many books currently on the market that fulfill this need.

This is a book for dog owners who wish to use a positive approach to dog training but do not wish to learn the science behind the method. It's written for people who simply want to see quick results. There will be little scientific terminology, and no history of clicker use or other psychological discussions that can get confusing. Instead, I will explain how to train a dog using a clicker, step by step, so that anyone—dog owner, new dog trainer, or experienced dog trainer—can easily understand and implement these methods.

Clicker training zeroes in on changing behavior, not changing the animal. It provides a clear and immediate consequence. Once understood, the method is fast, easy and, best of all, positive.

As I crossed over from traditional training to clicker training, I became enlightened. Not only did I learn how to reward the dog for doing something right instead of punishing him for doing something wrong, but I realized that this approach transfers to everyday living. It teaches us to look for the positive things in life: Reward the good things you see in both your pet and your family, because whatever is rewarded will be strengthened. Ignore the wrong behavior, because it is merely a means of garnering attention. What you ignore will fade away.

As you learn how to clicker train your dog, I hope you will also become enlightened to how much your dog can learn in a short period of time. There are no boundaries as far as abilities, age, or breed. Any dog can learn anything you wish to take the time to teach.

So, with a little imagination and a lot of patience . . .

Here we go!

Chapter 1

Get Clicked

Before you begin clicker training, you need to understand the underlying principles that make the clicker so effective. This knowledge will help you understand how to use the clicker and your dog learn how to react to it.

Basically, you will need to know three things:

1. What a clicker is and how it works
2. The effect this tool has on your dog and how it is used in the training process
3. How to use vocal tones and visual cues while training with a clicker

Understanding the ideas behind clicker training will also help you learn where and when clickers can be used in everyday canine activities. Clicker training is not just for basic obedience or problem solving. This tool is also used to teach working dogs their performance patterns. It opens up their ability to reason their way through obstacles and solve problems, as they figure out which behaviors would be rewarding and which will not.

WHAT IS A CLICKER?

A clicker is a noise-making device that was once a child's toy. The old ones are made entirely of metal and were often designed in bright colors and pleasing shapes, such as animals. To make the clicking noise, a flexible metal tongue in the middle is pressed down onto another piece of metal. The sound is best if the piece of metal is pressed and released quickly.

Clickers are currently made of plastic rectangular or oval boxes with a flexible metal piece in the middle that makes a distinctive sound. Clicker training has become so popular that you can obtain a clicker at most pet supply shops or from many catalogs and online stores.

A variety of clickers.

Even though they are mass-produced, each clicker has its own unique sound. Because dogs can hear far better than humans, they can tell the difference, no matter how slight. That means in a class full of dogs and clicker trainers, your dog can still pick out the sound of your clicker.

It also means a clicker does not need to be used directly under a dog's nose. In fact, it's best not to point it at the dog at all. You can keep it behind your back or in a pocket. A muffled click is easier to accept than a loud, sharp click. Some dogs are easily frightened by loud noises, and clicking under their noses will disrupt the learning processes.

The clicker is not a target for your dog to point his nose at. It's also not a remote control, although it can sometimes seem like one, because once your dog sees you pick up the clicker he'll start doing things, possibly even at random, to try to earn rewards.

Collars, leashes, whistles, treats, and toys are all tools that help in the training process. A clicker is as much a training aid as a collar and leash. It's not used in the same way, but does help you communicate with the dog. The proper use of these tools creates a happy, well-adjusted dog who loves to work with you.

The clicker can be used alone, without other training devices, or in conjunction with them. The need for various tools depends upon the dog and the situation. (I will describe several training tools and their advantages and disadvantages in chapter 2.) However, in most quiet surroundings, where there is little distraction, nothing will be required besides you, your dog, the clicker, and the reward. There will be no need to contain, force, or coerce your dog's performance.

It will happen.

WHY USE A CLICKER?

A clicker is a way of letting your dog know when he has done the right thing. It acts as a bridge between Teddy doing what he was told and receiving his reward. It is an efficient way of relating this information quickly and distinctively.

Once you understand how to use a clicker, it proves more efficient than using your voice. That's because your voice is always in use. This isn't a bad thing, because you will need to use varying tones and specific words to communicate with your dog. However, since your voice is a constant sound in your dog's life, it doesn't offer a distinctive sound to reinforce a good response. This is important, because Teddy will be less confused if he receives notice of a good behavior the moment it occurs. Telling him "good boy" as he moves away from doing something you want only rewards him for moving away, not for doing what you had requested.

Here's an example. Let's say you want Teddy to sit. He does so, but then jumps up on you, his muddy paws redesigning your apparel. You had praised him, but not at the exact moment he sat. He received his praise as he was rising up to jump on you. Teddy has learned that the act of jumping up on you is rewarding but the act of sitting is not; therefore, he will continue to jump on you. Had you clicked when he sat, he would have learned *that* behavior was what you wanted, because he was rewarded for it and the act of jumping was not rewarded. The result would be a dog who sits for a reward instead of jumping up for it.

As this example illustrates, verbal praise doesn't always come at the right time. It is far more difficult to express praise in the proper tone of voice than it is to simply press on the clicker. Yes, you always carry your voice with you, whereas you don't always carry a clicker. But eventually you won't need to carry the clicker because your dog will respond properly to vocal and visual cues. When teaching your dog something new, however, it's best to offer a timely bridge to his proper response, and the clicker works best for this.

The sound of the clicker offers a nonemotional response. Regardless of the mood you are in, your dog receives a consistent bridge, thereby producing reliability. You can use the clicker from any position, any location, and under any environmental conditions. You can be sitting, standing, near, or far. You can be inside, outside, in a quiet yard, or a busy shopping mall. Your dog will learn to work for the sound of the clicker because he knows the sound will be followed by a reward. His mind will be fixed on offering a proper response to your cues.

HOW IS A CLICKER USED IN DOG TRAINING?

A clicker marks the moment your dog has done something good. Through conditioning, your dog will learn that the sound of the click means he will receive a reward. The reward can be food, a toy, touch, or any number of other actions. While many dogs are happy to work for their kibble, not all of them prefer food rewards, though most will work for a piece of hotdog, liver, steak, cheese, or chicken. A favorite toy can be substituted for the food, as can a rub on the head or chest.

This dog is receiving a reward after a click.

When you teach your dog the meaning of a clicker, you need to stick to specific parameters. Changing your criteria will cause your dog to lose interest. The main parameter is that your dog receives a reward for every single click. Never click without giving your dog his reward.

You want for your dog to work for the sound, not ignore it. Giving him a reward each time will maintain his enthusiasm and motivation. It will also maintain clarity of communication between you and your dog. Think of it as making a deal with your dog: You must maintain your part of the bargain if you expect your dog to maintain his part.

There is a three-step pattern I use when teaching a dog.

1. Present a stimulus. A stimulus is something that will grab your dog's attention. A piece of food or a toy is a stimulus. To make the entire process easy, I use the stimulus as a lure. Once Teddy understands that you're holding something he wants, you can make him do anything. Your hand will become the stimulus, because it holds the lure.

2. As soon as Teddy pays attention to the stimulus and performs the correct action, click the clicker and praise.

3. Give Teddy the reward.

Lure, click, reward!

As your dog learns that the sound of the clicker means he will be receiving a reward, you will be able to gradually increase the time between the sound of the click and his receipt of the reward. However, maintain the deal you made with Teddy and always reward for every click.

As your dog learns the meaning of each cue (that is, each verbal command and/or visual signal), you will be able to reduce the use of the lure and replace it with a cue, thereby reducing the number of rewards given. When you get to this point, the sound of the clicker is in and of itself a reward.

USING VERBAL AND VISUAL CUES WITH A CLICKER

What is a cue? A cue is a signal that tells the dog to perform a specific command. This signal is learned by conditioning the dog to respond to it in a specific manner. The signal can be visual, verbal, or the presence of an object. If you don't know which to use, I'd suggest visual, because dogs are very visually oriented. As you progress, you can add verbal cues that can either mean the same thing or a different version of the behavior. For example, you can use a hand signal that means sit while also using the word. Or you can use the hand signal to mean sit in a specific location, while the word "sit" means merely to plop the rear wherever. The choice is yours, but always be consistent so you don't confuse yourself or your dog.

There is an art to using visual and verbal cues. The motion, or lack thereof, can help the dog quickly understand what you want. When using verbal cues, your tone also carries a lot of meaning. In fact, much can be communicated through body language and vocal tones. The ultimate goal of training is complete communication without the use of training aids.

The handler is giving a visual cue for the sit command.

Voice Cues

While many clicker trainers prefer *not* to use the voice to convey cues, I have *always* used my voice to instruct and guide my dogs. I have yet to meet a dog who did not enjoy hearing the voice of their human companion(s). I guide with my voice from the very start of any training session.

In the beginning, you only use your voice when praising the dog. This gives the dog positive associations with your voice. When your dog does something you wish, you click and praise, then give him the treat. The praise will then have worth when you dispense with the clicker.

Once your dog understands a specific behavior, such as sitting, you add the word, "sit." This is a cue. Offering the word after the dog understands the exercise ensures that the cue is associated with the correct action, instead of with something else.

Most dogs learn very quickly. You should be able to add your vocal cues within three or four repetitions. Here's an example, in which you are teaching Teddy to sit.

- He sits. You click and praise, then give him his reward.
- He sits again. You click and praise, then give him his reward.
- You repeat this four or five times.
- You say, "Teddy, sit." He sits. You click and praise, then give him his reward.

After four or five repetitions, Teddy will fully understand the word "sit." You can test this by moving to different locations and giving him the sit command (cue). If he sits, you click and praise, then give the reward. If not, it doesn't mean he's being bad; it's simply that he hasn't yet associated the cue with the action. The lack of response might also be due to a change in location. Go back to the beginning, remaining close to your dog and reinforcing the behavior through more repetitions. Then begin adding the cue again.

As you see, there is no correction involved, merely clear communication and patience as your dog figures out what you want. It sometimes takes a little time to wake up your dog's thinking and reasoning processes. Once Teddy's wheels start turning, though, they go faster and faster.

You may have noticed that I always precede the command with the dog's name. This is important, because not only does it teach the dog his name, but it also gets his attention before you give the command. The command should only be given one time, and getting the dog's attention helps him understand that you are speaking to him and want him to do something. When you say his name, use a "come hither" tone of voice. Never say his name in a scary or intimidating manner. You want Teddy to love hearing his name, not to run in the other direction.

When you begin teaching Teddy to associate the clicker with rewards, you begin by simply saying his name. When he looks at you, you click and praise, then give him his reward. Now he'll have positive associations with his name. It's also the start of teaching him to come to you when you call him. The mere mention of his name will grab his attention.

Think of this process as trying to teach your dog a new language. Dogs don't come into the world knowing our language. Teddy speaks canine. You speak human. Speaking loud and slow won't help him understand. You need to bridge the language gap by showing your dog the meaning of each word. Repeating the word merely makes him believe that he does not need to respond until you say it ten times. By luring him into a behavior, repeating the action a few times, then adding the word for the action, you are teaching him the meaning of the word in a positive, associative manner. Teddy will be happy to oblige.

When using verbal cues, be sure to use words that are clearly differentiated from one another. This will help your dog discern the meaning of each word. Here's a list of sample words to use throughout the training process:

Heel (to walk with you or sit at your side in heeling position)

Sit

Stay (regardless of the position, the verbal and visual cues remain the same)

Down

Come

Swing (to return to heel position)

Stand

For tricks, again use clear cues, such as shake, roll over, sit pretty, speak, find, get, take, drop, and so on. The shorter and more concise the word, the faster Teddy will understand the meaning.

As your dog learns several behaviors, you can string the verbal cues together to form a chain. For example, if you wish your dog to come to you, sit, and then bark, the verbal cues are, "Teddy come, sit, speak," in that order, since that is how you wish it done. If you want him to bark first, you'll need to give that cue first.

Canine Vocal Tones

Dogs also use their voices to convey information. There are a variety of canine tones and vocalizations, and they differ according to the breed(s) of the dog. Some dogs do a "roo roo," while others have an "arroo." Some dogs howl and others bray. Only a dog of the same breed knows the real message, but there are several vocalizations that are universal in the dog world. Emulating them as closely as possible while teaching Teddy our words aids in bridging the language barrier.

I use three distinct tones that are based on these canine vocal tones. The first is a high, happy, enthusiastic tone, which is used with praise. When giving a command, I use a demanding tone. This is the equivalent of a loud bark. Please note that the demanding tone need not be loud or stern. Dogs hear very well and will respond better to a softly spoken word than one that is loud and harsh. The third tone is a low, growly tone, for correction. With clicker training, there is very little correction involved; mostly, this involves redirection and clarification of a cue. Since dogs aren't spiteful or malicious, your dog simply may not fully understand what you requested. Thus, you'll accomplish far more if you clarify your command than if you punish your dog for not doing what you asked. A low tone merely lets the dog know he should try something different.

Dogs also use a whimpering tone that means they are scared, stressed, or seek attention. This is probably not a good tone to use at any time, because you want Teddy to see you as leader of his pack, not as an injured, frightened puppy.

Visual Cues

Dogs are very visually oriented and communicate with subtle visual cues. From the way they position their eyes, ears, and mouth to the level of their tails, every body movement has a distinct meaning. Using visual cues during training makes for clear communication. The tricky part will be teaching your dog to identify with the visual cues you *wish* to present, as opposed those you *accidentally* present. For example, suppose you wish your dog to identify the down command with your pointing downward. He not only sees that hand cue, but also how you are holding your body, the expression on your face, and the distractions around him. To be perfectly clear on the cue, you need to minimize as many other visual cues as you can. Begin the training in a quiet place and do lots of repetitions.

A visual cue for the down command.

When you start training a visual cue, use a large, easy-to-understand signal. For example, when teaching your dog to lie down, don't just point downward but also lean over, looking at your dog. Some handlers may bend at the knees (especially when working with a small dog). This, too, becomes part of the dog's cue. Your entire body is conveying the cue for the down command.

As with verbal commands, you want to keep your visual cues distinct and clear. Whether you're using a visual cue close to your dog or from a distance, it's best to keep the cue away from the silhouette of your body. Dogs do not see details from a distance. Unless you're very close by, few can see the expression on your face, or arm movement when your arm is held close to your body. They see motion and shape. Therefore, while you are teaching your dog the language of cues, signs that can be used from *any* distance are more consistent than changing the cues due to distance.

The more simple the presentation, the faster your dog learns. The more consistent you are, the more reliable your dog will become.

If you wish to teach Teddy to rely on facial expressions or very small motions for his cues, you can use these in conjunction with the bigger, clearer signals that you'll be using from a distance. In other words, present both. With repetition, your dog can learn to perform the same behavior from a variety of visual cues. For example, you can use a finger pointing downward for the down command and then a hand held high when requesting the behavior from a distance. To make the entire process easier, you might want to use both cues as you teach the behavior, so your dog will learn right from the start to respond to either of them.

Examples of Visual Cues

On the next few pages you'll find suggestions for visual cues. I use these particular cues because they have worked for me and are always clear to the dog. Feel free to discover visual cues that are comfortable for your own use. Just remember to keep the signal clear while offering a visual guide to the behavior you are requesting.

Come. Face your dog, hold your hand to your side, treat within, and bend at the waist. If this is too intimidating for your dog, bend at the knees. (Eventually you will be able to do this standing up and with your hand empty, as shown here.). Bring your hand in toward you . . .

. . . in a welcoming motion, until your palm is flat against your chest.

Sit. Stand upright. Show your dog the treat (the target), then lift it between Teddy's eyes, just out of reach. This will eventually be turned into the more distinct motion shown here of lifting your hand from the elbow, palm up.

Down. Bend at the waist. Using your index finger, point all the way to the floor with one hand. You can reach into the air with the other (not shown here), so that the hand reaching into the air will be the distance signal for down.

Stay. Extend your hand with fingers spread, open palm facing the dog. This signal can be used for sit-stay, down-stay, stand-stay, or to signal the dog to stop and stay from a motion behavior. Consistency with the cue helps the dog understand the meaning far better than changing the cue according to the position or the amount of time you wish him to remain in position.

Go left. Your right hand is stretched outward and points to your right—the dog's left.

Go right. Your left hand is stretched outward and points to your left—the dog's right.

Lift left leg. Bend your right arm (the dog's left side as you face him) at the elbow, at a ninety-degree angle from your side.

Lift right leg. Bend your left arm (the dog's right side as you face him) at the elbow, at a ninety-degree angle from your side.

Sit up. Closed fist, with your index finger lifted upward.

Give. Hand held low, cupped, with the palm facing upward.

Wrong. Turn your back on your dog, nose in the air, arms crossed.

Good/Yes. With a smile on your face and your body bent slightly at the waist, clap your hands softly.

Canine Body Language

Understanding what your dog is telling you is a big part of bridging the communication gap. We expect our dogs to learn our language, and we must also make an effort to learn theirs. Since the majority of their communication is through body language, let's take a quick look at the canine signals that pertain to the training process.

- Ears forward, eyes wide open, tail held upward but not stiffly: attentive.
- Ears back a little, eyes blinking, tail held down: intimidated.
- Body very low, belly to the ground, ears flat back, neck stretched: very frightened. (Please take note that approaching a dog showing this behavior can be dangerous. More dogs bite out of fear than outright aggression.)
- Rolled over onto the back, tail tucked between the legs, teeth showing, eyes turned away: extremely frightened and showing submission.
- Watching you, ears swiveling around, tail wagging slowly: slightly distracted but listening to you.
- Lifting legs high while walking: a happy worker.
- Body held low while walking, tail between legs, eyes blinking: frightened or upset.
- Front end on the ground, back end up in the air, tail wagging, sometimes also barking: inviting play.
- Sit, lie down, roll over, bark, lift paw, back up and any number of other behaviors: throwing out behaviors to see which one will earn him a click and reward. This is a dog who is thinking!

PERFORMING ARTS

Not only does clicker training help with basic obedience and overall good manners, it can also be used to teach advanced behaviors such as tricks, service work, and many types of performance sports. Regardless of the type of work—obedience, agility, rally-o, assistance dogs, or performing in the media—professional handlers are using clickers to reinforce their dogs' good behavior.

Obedience, Agility, and Rally-O

These activities require a dog to execute commands quickly and precisely. The dog must perform both on and off leash, heeling, stays, recall (come when called), sit, down, finish (return to the heel position), retrieve, directed jumping, scent discrimination, go in a specific direction, and more.

While preparing a dog for any type of performance trial, the clicker is used to reinforce each part of the individual exercises. For example, to teach a dog to heel the handler breaks down the behavior into smaller components. Every dog must learn to walk one step at a time, just like a baby. As the dog accomplishes each minor step, he is reinforced until he understands the entire behavior. From the dog meandering around off leash as his handler is walking, to guiding him using clicker training into the perfect heeling position, the dog is brought through the exercise click by click, step by step.

Assistance Work

Guide dogs for the blind, alert dogs, service dogs, and hearing dogs (among assistance dogs) must *want* to work. It's very difficult to rely on an assistance dog who has been forced into obedience, because he becomes fearful when he works incorrectly. It is important that the dog work regardless of the circumstances; he can't be stymied by one wrong move. A clicker-trained dog is never fearful of being wrong. He merely keeps trying.

For example, a guide dog works every day, all day, and must reason through problems while knowing a goal. A guide dog must cross the street, leading his partner, without getting hit by a car. The dog must be aware of oncoming traffic and guide his partner around obstacles and other people along the way.

A guide dog has to be aware of many factors, not just one cue from his handler. Let's say the guide dog notices that the traffic has stopped and begins crossing the street with his partner. Suddenly, a person stops directly ahead or a vehicle begins to move forward. The dog knows to move far enough away from the person/car to avoid having his handler or himself bump into it. There was a sudden change and the dog had to quickly reason through it. Many dogs who have been trained using punishment might try to avoid the problem instead of adjusting to it, in which case the dog would have dragged his handler back to the corner and stayed there. A clicker-trained dog learns that he must simply keep trying until he presents the correct response.

Watching an assistance dog such as a guide dog work can help you understand a dog's keen awareness of his environment. The slightest change in anything can elicit an entirely different reaction from the dog. This can also help you understand how important it is to teach your dog to work in the presence of all kinds of distractions (this is known as distraction proofing).

Clicker training is also very helpful when working with search and rescue dogs and police dogs, because a dog who can be guided in a specific manner is very useful. For example, a search and rescue dog who has been sent to look for missing people can be directed to look upward or down into a hole instead of merely following his nose or going forward. Wind direction and environmental factors greatly influence the direction of scent, and having a dog who is thorough and can search all niches has proven very helpful in locating people covered with debris or hiding near a ceiling.

Dogs with obsessive behaviors may also show deviations in behavior when their environment changes. Rizzo, a Cocker Spaniel I had the pleasure of knowing, had severe separation anxiety. If one little thing was moved or changed within his environment, he would push and bark at it until it was restored to its original state. While visiting with Rizzo on one occasion, I noticed he was poking and barking at an empty CD case near the fireplace. His owners explained that their housekeeper had placed it there when she stopped by while they were out of town. Upon returning, Rizzo made a complete circuit of his home, then stopped at the CD case and hadn't stopped poking at it since. Rizzo was merely pointing out that his environment had changed. To a person, this was so minor as to be barely noticeable, and in fact, Rizzo's owners hadn't noticed the wayward CD case until Rizzo pointed it out.

Media Dogs

I have had the pleasure of providing dogs for media productions since 1983. Teddy, the name I'm using to represent all dogs in this book, was one of my favorite canine actors. I have always found it helpful to use positive reinforcement while working on a production. One must have a happy, willing dog when working in the high-stress environment of filming a television commercial, feature film, or video. The use of force or coercion merely sets up the dog for failure and encourages an attitude of disregard for the process.

Up until recently, I used the word "good" as a bridging signal. (I still do when a clicker isn't handy.) Luckily, my timing is usually very good and dogs love to hear my voice because my praise is very enthusiastic and they know a treat is on its way. In addition my "good dog" stands out from the normal conversational tone on the set.

The clicker works the same way. Clickers carry a distinctive sound over a long distance, regardless of ambient noise and environmental conditions. This is important when you're working in the high-distraction environment of a media production. The canine actor must watch his handler at all times—not the cameraman, director, lighting engineer, gaffer, or production assistant.

Have you ever watched a program that features a dog and seen how he appears to look *through* the actor he is supposed to be looking *at*? This dog is looking at his handler, who is giving him his cues. He has learned that he must perform a chain of behaviors when the cues are given in order to receive his click and reward. He has been conditioned through positive training; thus, he doesn't stop after doing only one or two behaviors. He will continue to perform until he hears his bridging signal (the sound that tells him he has completed his actions)—the click. He is very reliable on his lines. The dog wrangler (production terminology for the handler) is like a big cue card for the dog.

In the spring of 2001, my Australian Shepherd Sydney and I worked at the Landsburgh Theater in Washington, D.C., in a production of the musical version of *Two Gentlemen of Verona*. The theater had more than 500 seats, but none of the actors used microphones because the stage sound carried well throughout the theater. I could not be seen by the audience, nor heard by the dog. I had to rely upon her desire to keep her eyes on me while the production went on around her.

Attentiveness was never an issue for Sydney, and she was an acting veteran by this time. She was 13, and had been performing in productions her entire life. People would often try to get her to come to them or even look at them, but she never would. Her eyes were always glued on me.

I was placed in the stage wings with a small light over me so that, out of the blackness, Sydney could see my silhouette. I had to use visual cues that were very distinct and away from my body. I used my left hand in the air for down, a bend forward for come, and my right hand raised from the elbow, palm up, for sit. Another, more difficult, behavior was speak. She had to perform this at exactly the right moment. This meant giving the cue fifteen seconds before that moment. I used the cue of lifting my right hand to my right ear as I leaned forward.

A further complication was my having to cross behind the stage to the other side to cue Sydney to come off stage. Rehearsals helped prepare her for my location switch, so that by show time she knew where to expect me and when.

After a week of performances, Sydney knew the pattern and no longer waited for my visual cues. In fact, she started adding her own little extras, such as yawning at the most comedic moment and starting to leave the stage before her acting companion was ready. Luckily, the actor was also able to improvise. All in all, the audience had a good laugh, and Sydney would wiggle her rear with excitement.

Due to the commotion and distraction, a production dog must be able to discern a very small cue as meaningful, while all else in the environment has no effect on his behavior. This takes many training sessions, including distraction proofing and location proofing. While some dogs can perform in this type of situation from puppyhood, others are not able to until they are well over two years of age.

Dogs who learn to work for a click learn faster and are far more distraction proofed than those trained with traditional methods. A dog trained through positive reinforcement has a happy demeanor. He will continue performing regardless of how many takes (repeated scene performances) the director asks for—and there is always more than one take in every aspect of a production, which means the canine actor invariably has to perform the same chain of behaviors more than five or ten times in succession. A clicker-trained dog will display enthusiasm throughout the filming session.

So from now on, when you see animals in the media, you will know that they are looking at their target (either their trainer or an object they've been trained to look at), and performing a chain of behaviors that has been conditioned through positive reinforcement. Most canine wranglers in the production business use clickers (or some other form of bridging signal) and rewards to obtain optimum performances from their furry, four-footed actors.

Regardless of your goals for *your* Teddy, you can achieve them using the procedures detailed in this book.

Let's begin!

Chapter 2

The Basics in Basic Language

There are several techniques you need to know about before starting any clicker training program. They are the basics for all that follows. First, you must accustom your dog to the sound of the clicker and teach him that the sound means a reward is coming. Second, you need to teach your dog to target, either to your hand or a target stick.

Once you and Teddy are familiar with the timing and reward delivery of the clicker, you will learn about how to shape a behavior. This means that you guide your dog from not knowing something to understanding it in detail with a high rate of reliability.

Clicker training alone in a quiet environment is a great way to begin, but this is not real life. The real world is filled with distractions. There are many distractions that are more inviting than food or toy rewards. The mere presence of a gate or a door may be far more important to Teddy than a piece of steak. How can a piece of hotdog compare with the thrill of chasing a squirrel?

You can't always have full control over your dog's behavior. This is why training tools must be used. There is a great variety from which to choose. In this chapter I will describe the most popular ones on the market and how to use them. If your dog does not respond quickly to their use, consult with a professional trainer. It could be that you are not using the tool correctly or it is the wrong tool for your dog.

As much as clicker trainers want to approach dog training with only positive reinforcement (using only rewards, never punishment), it is rare that this works 100 percent of the time on 100 percent of dogs. Clicker training gurus Gary Wilkes and Karen Pryor recommend using training tools as aids. These tools don't always have to be used as punishment; they can also be used for redirection. Training tools help guide your dog through the rough spots.

Let's say you are out walking with a friend who is from out of the country and doesn't speak your language very well. She sees something in a store window that grabs her attention. She says something in her language, but you don't understand, so you keep walking. She grabs your arm and pulls you to the store window. She guided you where she wanted by applying something aversive: a pull. It wasn't a severe punishment, merely a means of guidance. Next time you might be watching her a little better and listening for those specific words, just in case something else catches her eye.

Your friend used a training tool: her hand on your arm, pulling. Had you been wearing a neck collar and leash, it would've been far more convenient for your friend. Dogs see the quick approach of a hand and/or body as a threatening gesture. It is far less threatening to them for you to pull on a leash than to grab for their neck or collar. That's why leashes are great training tools.

CLICK & TREAT

Click and treat is the very first step to clicker training. You must teach Teddy that the sound of the clicker means he'll be receiving a reward. For the sake of consistency (yes, I like to use this word a lot; it is key to successful training), let's use a treat as the reward. Freeze-dried liver, which is my training treat *du jour*, is not turned down by many dogs.

Before you begin, make sure you have the tools you need:

- A clicker.
- A treat pouch filled with treats.
- A quiet, enclosed training area.
- Don't forget your dog!

Charge It!

The following sequence will quickly teach your dog to associate the sound of the clicker with the fact that he will be rewarded.

1. Place some treats on the floor near you.
2. As Teddy goes to the treats, click. Click for each treat he eats.
3. Put a few treats on the floor in another part of the room. Click for each treat he eats.
4. Show Teddy the treats in your hand. (We don't want to establish that all the treats come from the floor or Teddy will be watching the floor instead of you, so we now begin to correlate that the treats come from you.)

5. Click and give him a treat.

6. Do this four more times. (By now Teddy has a very good understanding that the click means he's getting a treat. In fact, you might start seeing him salivate.)

7. Let's test Teddy's knowledge. Go to another part of the room and click. Teddy will immediately look at you. As he does so, toss him his treat.

Go do something else for a while. Read a book, watch television, do the dishes. Observe Teddy and note that he's keeping an eye on you. He has learned that good things come from you. He might even start trying out behaviors at random to try to earn that click again. Don't give in to this, or you'll be trained by Teddy! Don't allow him to tell you when to begin training sessions.

When you're ready, return to the quiet room or enclosure and do the clicker association work again. Or, if Teddy is ignoring other things in the environment, see how well he does with a few more distractions. It may take only one or two five-minute training sessions to teach your dog to associate the sound of the clicker with a treat.

TARGETING

Ideally, you want Teddy to begin by targeting on your hand. It is far easier to have him touch a hand that holds a treat than to touch an inanimate object that holds the promise of a treat. The smell of the treat is a quicker way to get his attention. Your hand will also guide Teddy into the sit, down, heel, and more. Later, you'll learn how to teach your dog to target a stick or other inanimate object.

An important part of targeting is luring. The lure is the reward—in this case, a piece of freeze-dried liver held within your hand. When Teddy touches his nose to your hand, you click, praise, and give him his treat.

Here's a quick way to teach your dog to target your hand.

1. Show Teddy the hand that has the reward inside. He will sniff it.

2. As he sniffs, click and praise.

3. Give him the treat.

4. To be sure Teddy understands that your hand is the target, you're going to move it around a bit. Start by moving your hand to the left.

5. As Teddy follows your hand, click and praise.

6. Give him the treat.

7. Move your hand to the right.

8. As Teddy follows your hand, click and praise.

9. Give him the treat.

You've got the pattern by now. Add more, such as moving your hand both left and right, or up and down. Each time your dog's nose follows your hand, click, praise, and treat.

Now your dog understands how to target.

To move away from having to lure your dog into targeting, do the following:

1. Make a fist and then hold your hand down where Teddy can smell it.

2. When he puts his nose near your hand, click and praise.

3. Give him the reward with your other hand.

4. Repeat two or three times.

Teddy has learned that the treat may not be in the hand he's pointing to, but the act of pointing to the hand still earns him the reward. Now your dog will target your hand without you having to hold treats in that hand.

Luring with treats will play a large part in teaching many new behaviors, so it is an important skill to reinforce throughout the training process.

Target an Object

There are several ways to teach your dog to target an inanimate object. The first is to place a treat near or on top of the object. In this case we'll use a target stick, but keep in mind the target can be anything you wish. The sequence goes like this.

1. Have someone hold your dog securely as you place a treat near the target. If you don't have the luxury of having someone hold your dog, place him in another area as you set up the target and treat.

2. Allow your dog to go to the target stick and sniff.

3. As he finds his reward, click and praise.

4. Repeat this at least four times.

5. Wait for Teddy to touch the stick without your having placed a treat near it. Don't worry, he will. Be patient.

Place the treat near the target stick.

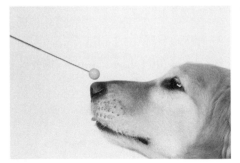

Wait until your dog sniffs the target stick, then click and treat.

6. As he touches the stick, click and praise.

7. Give him his treat.

8. Repeat this four times or more and you'll have Teddy touching the object to get his click, because he knows the reward follows.

Now you can repeat this exercise with other objects. Use a plastic lid, a ball, a bone, or whatever else you want. As Teddy learns to touch a target object, begin naming the object. Then you can start playing the Touch It game, where you tell your dog to touch a specific item that you name. Here's how you play.

1. Let's say you are using a ball and a bone. Place both items on the floor.

2. Tell him to touch the ball. Wait patiently. Don't do or say anything to guide him.

3. The second he goes near the ball, click and praise. Give him his reward.

4. Repeat this a second and third time, always with the ball.

5. Next, tell him to go for his bone. Again, wait until he goes near it. Then click, praise, and reward.

6. Repeat this a few more times.

7. Now you can rotate between the two objects, with Teddy having a full understanding of the names of each toy and that you wish him to go to them on command.

It's not difficult to teach your dog to target a ball.

You can teach your dog to target a squeaky toy.

The second way of teaching Teddy to target something other than your hand is through behavior shaping. You are forming his desire to touch the inanimate object by teaching him that it is rewarding. It's similar to the game Hot and Cold you played as a child. As you came near the selected object, the person who was "it" said "hot," and when you moved away from the object, they said "cold." You just did this same thing with the Touch It game.

Now you can use this concept to teach Teddy any behavior you wish.

BEHAVIOR SHAPING

Behavior shaping is done by breaking down any skill you wish to teach into easy-to-learn increments. Some parts may be learned quickly, while others may take a little longer. If learning one part of the skill seems to take too long, you can always break that down into even smaller parts. Keep in mind that if your dog doesn't respond it doesn't mean he's being disobedient; he simply doesn't understand what you want.

Let's teach targeting through behavior shaping. First, we need to break down the behavior into smaller increments. We begin with a dog who doesn't know what to touch. We wish to end with the dog touching his nose to the end of a target stick. In the middle are the following steps:

1. Teddy looks at the target stick.
2. He moves his upper body toward the target stick.
3. He moves his hind legs toward the target stick.
4. He moves a few feet toward the target stick.
5. He is next to the target stick.
6. He reaches out his nose toward the target stick.
7. He touches the stick with his nose.
8. He touches the end of the stick with his nose.
9. He repeats the exercise a couple times.
10. You add the command "Touch the stick."

Each time your dog does one of the steps above, you click, praise, and give him his treat. If he does not complete any step, go back to the last step he clearly understood and repeat it a few times, then continue on to the next step. With most dogs, however, this process will happen far more quickly than you can imagine, and you will end up skipping some of these steps as Teddy quickly understands what you want.

Now that Teddy understands how to touch a target stick, you can use this tool to guide him to touch other objects or go to a specific location. Here's an exercise you can try to test his knowledge.

1. Place the target stick next to a squeaky toy.
2. Tell Teddy "touch."
3. As he touches the target stick, click, praise, and give him his treat.
4. Repeat this at least three times.
5. Take away the target stick but leave the squeaky toy. Tell Teddy "touch" (don't add the name of the object yet). At first he might be confused because the target stick is no longer there. But eventually he will start in the direction of the squeaky toy. As he does, click, praise, and give him his treat.

"Touch squeaky." No problem!

6. Wait until he goes nearer to the squeaky toy. Click, praise, and give him his treat.

7. Continue shaping him into touching the squeaky toy. Each time he makes progress, click, praise, and reward. Teddy will probably be touching the squeaky toy faster than you can read these directions.

8. Now that Teddy understands you want him to touch the squeaky toy, add the name of the toy to the command: "touch squeaky."

Let's test your dog's knowledge by going to a different location to touch the squeaky toy.

1. Move the squeaky toy a short distance away from you, say about four feet.

2. Instruct Teddy to "touch squeaky."

3. He'll most likely do so. If not, gradually shape the behavior by clicking when he looks at it, takes a step toward it, and so on, until he reaches and touches the toy.

4. Move the squeaky toy to a new location. Repeat the exercise.

5. Teddy will soon understand the game and will leap across the room to touch the toy wherever you place it.

Next, try using a different object. If, at any time, your dog appears confused, gradually shape his attention onto the new object in the same way as you did the target stick and the squeaky toy. This game can evolve into your teaching Teddy to touch specific people, as well. This can get really interesting; eventually, the people can "hide" throughout the house or the yard and you can send Teddy to go find them.

The lure makes it easy to get the dog into the sit position.

With each new behavior you teach, you can either lure the dog or shape the behavior. I like to use both methods at the same time, because this makes for faster, more successful training.

For example, when teaching your dog to sit, you can lure him into the proper position and use your clicker to mark the moment that position is achieved. After a couple of repetitions, you add the cue word and reduce the lure to your hand signal. You click, praise, and then present your dog with his reward.

This can usually be done in a few minutes with most dogs, so make sure you are completely comfortable with the procedures and are ready to quickly adapt to your dog's learning curve.

Another fun exercise to practice shaping was developed by Karen Pryor and is called 101 Things to Do with a Box. This is the perfect behavior-shaping game, because there are so many things you can do with it. Do you remember how much fun you had as a child when something came in a big box? You could make it into a fort, part of a Halloween costume, a secret hide-a-way, or a boat in which you could sail the oceans. Your dog can have fun the same way!

Take a low-sided box and place it in the middle of the floor. Allow Teddy to investigate the new object. As he moves close to it, click, praise, and reward. Each time he moves closer, click, praise, and reward.

Now that you have Teddy targeting the box, what next? How about teaching him to place all four feet inside the box? Let's break this down into small increments. (Remember, you will click, praise, and treat after each step.)

1. Teddy touches the box with his nose. If you wish to expedite this part, put a treat near the box or point to it with the target stick; Teddy is certain to pay attention to it.

2. He moves close enough for one of his front legs to touch the box.

3. He puts a foot inside the box.

4. He puts both front legs inside the box.

5. He moves toward the middle of the box with both front legs.

Targeting the box.

One foot inside the box.

Both front legs inside the box.

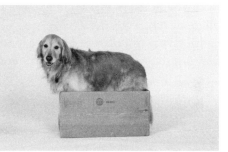

All four legs inside the box.

6. One hind leg enters the box.

7. Both hind legs enter the box. Now all four legs are inside the box.

Always be very observant of Teddy's movements. Each time he accomplishes the step, require more of him, gently guiding him to the next step. Depending on your dog and your training skills, this entire process may take a few sessions to accomplish, or, if your dog is highly motivated and your timing is very accurate, you may accomplish the entire thing in just ten minutes.

What else can you do with the box? Remember, there are 101 things you can do, and I've only named 8 of them. Teddy can learn to fetch it, take it somewhere, put things in it, and take things out of it. The list goes on as far as your imagination can take you. Any dog can have fun and learn with behavior shaping.

USING TRAINING TOOLS

Few dogs can go through the entire training process without you using a collar, leash, or other training tool. Dogs are predators and they are born with a prey drive. Movement, sound, or the smell of something enticing will distract them. Plus, there are very few urban, suburban, or even rural places without leash laws that require your dog to wear a collar or a harness and a leash. You must acclimate Teddy to these tools and teach him that he should not pull against them.

Each tool will apply pressure in different ways. Your dog's reaction to this pressure will determine whether the tool will be useful or ineffective. Regardless of the tool you use, you must continue to use positive reinforcement with the clicker and rewards. Remember that the ultimate goal is to have a dog who is reliable using verbal and visual communication alone, without the use of *any* training tool.

Flat Collar

Nearly every dog has a regular flat collar. This can be made of a variety of materials: cotton, leather, nylon, or neoprene. The collar either buckles closed or has a clip for quick release. Most have a D-ring for attaching a leash. Identification, license, and rabies tags are often attached to the D-ring. Dogs wear these collars all day, every day.

It's very convenient to simply clip the leash on the flat collar as you are on your way out the door with your dog. But once you cross the threshold, Teddy becomes

a different animal. No longer is he watching you, trying out behaviors for a click. Instead, he's intent on catching that squirrel he's been watching, or catching up with the child on the bicycle who just passed. Instantly, he's at the end of the leash and you're pulling back, cutting off his air as the flat collar presses against his trachea. The more you do this, the more permanent damage you are causing to his trachea and laryngeal tubes. The damage is irre-

The collar on the left is nylon web and the one on the right is rolled leather.

versible without expensive surgery. Have you ever heard a dog coughing and gagging while it's being walked? That's a dog who has been damaged by neck restraint.

Flat collars are *not* training tools. Pulling on a flat collar merely restrains your dog with brute force. On occasion, a slight yank and release might work to grab your dog's attention, but only if the dog is very small. It's fine to attach your dog's leash to a flat collar once you have a reliable, well-trained dog who rarely pulls for any reason. Until then, don't do so.

Body Harness

Body harnesses are also restraint devices. Although a body harness rarely causes physical injury, it does not teach a dog to pay attention. Dogs naturally pull against pressure, and a body harness applies pressure regardless of its use. The slightest pull back is pressure. Most people will have to apply more muscle with this tool than any other training device.

If you must tie out your dog for a short period of time, the body harness is best. For traveling, the body harness can be used in conjunction with a seat belt. If you are involved in pulling activities, such as dog sledding or weight pulling, the harness is best because the dog can push into it and the pressure of the weight is evenly distributed through his upper body.

This body harness is for a small dog.

Choke Collar

There are several types of choke collars and many methods of using them. The nylon collar is placed just behind the ears and jaw. If a dog is being shown in a conformation dog show, it may be used to remind the dog to hold his head up. However, this is a means of forcing the dog to comply, rather than teaching him to do so. Most conformation handlers teach their dog to hold his head up by using lures. The collar is merely there to attach the handler to the dog while going around the show ring.

The nylon choke collar is often used by dog trainers to turn the dog's upper body around when he is looking elsewhere.

Choke chains are also used for their jerking action. When the dog doesn't listen, the leash is yanked, causing the collar to constrict. The collars I had used as a traditional trainer (which were developed by Barbara Woodhouse)

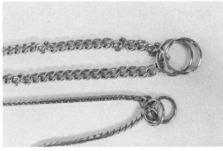

Two choke chain collars of different sizes.

made a jingling sound. This added sound grabbed the dog's attention without having to apply as much pressure to the leash jerk, but no choke collar works without some constriction.

Ideally, the collar is very briefly constricted and released, giving the dog a reminder to pay attention. However, this is still a tool for coercive, punishment-based training. When you are training with positive reinforcement, a choke collar is never necessary.

Martingale Collar

A martingale collar is a combination of a flat collar and a choke collar, in which the choke mechanism is limited. Martingale collars may be made entirely of metal

Martingale collars come in nylon web (left), chain, or a combination of the two (right).

chain, nylon web with a metal chain attachment, or entirely of nylon webbing. Unlike a choke chain, where the chain can be pulled very tight, the Martingale collar is limited by the length of the loop that attaches to the leash. The loop varies in length depending on the size of the collar, but it never tightens enough to choke the dog. However, it can apply pressure in much the same way as a flat collar.

This type of tool is fine for dogs who rarely pull. For instance, something attracts your dog's attention but a little tug on the leash, redirection from you, along with a click, praise, and reward, is all that's required to get back his focus. This is not a good tool for dogs who do a lot of pulling or are easily distracted. As with a choke chain and flat collar, it can cause physical damage if the dog pulls a lot.

Sense-sation and Easy Walk Harnesses

The Sense-sation and Easy Walk harnesses guide the front of the dog's body. It is placed around the shoulders and chest, with the leash ring at the center of the chest,

The Sense-sation harness offers an alternative to pulling at the dog's neck, because the leash is attached at his chest.

instead of over the back as with a regular body harness.

This tool offers an alternative to pulling against the dog's neck to redirect him. With all the pressure applied to the dog's chest, there's little chance of injury. These harnesses are great tools for a dog who is easily distracted but also easily redirected through positive guidance.

The harness must fit securely with little movement and should be used with a taut leash. Initially, the leash is attached to both a flat collar and the harness. As the dog acclimates to the harness, which can take from three to fourteen days, the leash is attached only to the O-ring at the dog's chest (as shown in the photo).

This training tool is used by pulling the leash in the opposite direction of the dog's pull. The manufacturer, and most dog trainers, suggest you have your dog walking on your left side. So if your dog pulls to the left, you pull the leash across his chest and turn to the right. Through right turns of 90 and 180 degrees, the dog will learn to pay attention. When turning left, lay the leash against the dog's neck and push the leash to your left. When you want your dog to stop or sit, you pull up until the dog complies. Add in the clicker and he will learn faster.

When using the harness off leash, the manufacturer suggests grabbing the chest strap at the dog's shoulder, as this offers more control. The action of correcting for not stopping or sitting is similar to that used with a leash: take hold of the chest strap and tug upward.

This harness should not be used with a jerk on the leash correction, as it does little besides annoy your dog. Nobody likes a nag, and dogs learn to tune out the jerking. Used correctly, though, the Sense-sation and Easy Walk harnesses are great learning tools.

Head Halter

Head halters were initially designed for dogs by Alice DeGroot, DVM, in the late 1970s for Irish Wolfhounds she had rescued. Because they are the size of small horses, she used the same device she'd use on a horse—a halter. She called her halter the K9 Kumalong. This head halter worked very well in reducing the leverage and pulling power of many large dogs.

The concept DeGroot used is known as a conventional design because it is very similar to the halter used on a horse. No pressure is applied unless the handler presses downward on the leash, which is attached to a ring under the dog's chin.

Another design, the figure-8, came on the market in the 1980s. It also offers the user better leverage on a pulling dog. However, with this design the nose strap must be clamped tightly around the jaw, causing much distress to many dogs. This constant pressure also means constant punishment. The dog can't get away from it by doing what has been requested by his handler. While some dogs quickly

I developed the Comfort Trainer head halter, a conventional head halter based upon Dr. Alice DeGroot's original design.

The Halti is another conventional head halter, also based upon DeGroot's original design. It was patented by Dr. Roger Mugford.

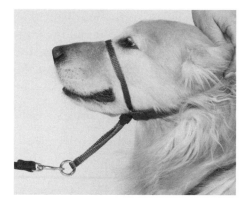

The Gentle Leader is a figure-8 head halter.

acclimate, many do not. In my opinion, the only reason this type of head halter should be used is for a very aggressive dog who can easily slip out of a conventional head halter.

There are several other head halters on the market, but these three are the most widely available. The Halti and Gentle Leader can be found at most pet supply superstores. The Comfort Trainer can be obtained from professional dog trainers, veterinarians, specialty pet supply shops, or on the Internet.

Head halters use the same idea as a dominant dog correcting a submissive dog. Pressure on the top of the muzzle, along with a growl, demonstrates dominance and correction. When you press on the dog's muzzle, the dog submits. In this book I won't go into the science behind this, but suffice it to say that properly applied pressure creates a cooperative dog who will not be easily distracted or assertive.

With a conventional head halter, the leash attaches to a ring hanging under the dog's chin. You hold the leash loosely in your right hand and place the clicker over the leash (see the photo below). The target is your left hand, which must either

Hold the leash loosely in your right hand and place the clicker over the leash.

Your left hand will be the dog's target, so it should be free or hold a reward.

hold a reward or simply be present as a clear cue. Therefore, no leash or clicker should be held in that hand.

When a head halter is used properly, there is rarely a need for correction. The real world, however, is filled with distractions far more enticing than the rewards you offer. The head halter will help you reinforce your wishes, even in the presence of distractions, in a way your dog understands.

For example, when you are walking and your dog moves ahead of you, regardless of the reason, pull downward with your right hand as you turn in the opposite direction. The second Teddy is looking at you and walking at your side, release the leash pressure, click, praise, and reward.

A head halter correction for forging ahead.

The head halter can also be used when a dog will not sit or rises out of a Sit-Stay. Pressure is applied under the chin using a gentle forward and upward pull. This brings the head up, thereby pressing the rear down. The moment this happens, the pressure under the dog's chin is released. Then simply click to mark the moment, praise, and reward.

Keep in mind that pulling down on the head halter is a form of punishment for not paying attention to you. Punishment should be associated with your correction word, "no," or "wrong." Eventually you will not have to apply nose pressure with a head halter to tell your dog to try something else; the word alone will be enough.

Head halters are marvelous for training aggressive dogs. As the dog feels the pressure on his nose, the desire to be assertive decreases. One can see the change in his eyes as the dominant stare

A head halter correction for not sitting.

turns into a more agreeable, softer eye. The dominant dog becomes more amenable to training and is easier to control if you encounter a major distraction.

Many head halter users claim the head halter is a "magic pill," giving them complete control in all situations. Head halters are great training tools, but they are not for all dogs. The only way to find out if a head halter is appropriate for your dog is to try one.

Before using a head halter, please consult with a professional trainer or read a book specifically about their use. If a head halter is not used correctly, the dog's spinal column can be severely damaged. Once the spinal column is traumatized, any number of structural and internal dysfunctions follow. By following these three rules, you will reduce the chance of injuring your dog.

1. Never pull your dog's head up and to the side.
2. Never allow the dog to pull on the halter as he would a harness. (This is not a *restraining* device; it is a *training* tool.)
3. Keep the leash loose, briefly applying pressure only when your dog will not target or pay attention to you.

POSITIVE CONTROL

Using the clicker, your target, and cues are positive ways to control your dog. Be sure to work on the timing of the clicker sound by practicing the games in this chapter before doing any formal work with your dog. You want Teddy to think the entire training process is a game, not a forced march.

Be creative and look for the good things. Click when they happen.

Chapter 3

Let's Begin

We'll start the training course with basic behaviors that will be used in nearly everything you do with Teddy. For example, you use sit to teach him to stay or lie down. He must know "down" if you wish him to stay for long periods of time. And he must know "stand" to receive proper care, such as physical examinations, bathing, grooming, and many other activities that are based on this position. Once Teddy can perform these three stationary behaviors, we'll move on to behaviors that involve motion, the heel and recall (another word for coming when called).

The stationary behaviors are easier to teach first, because you can do the training in any position *you* wish: sitting, standing, facing, or not facing your dog. Targeting maintains Teddy's attention throughout, making the entire process fast and easy.

Motion behaviors require you to use specific body language to aid your dog's learning process. These movements become part of the cues you'll use to communicate with your dog. Using specific, clear cues aids the learning and retention process.

When Teddy knows his basics, we'll teach him to stay in any position. A solid stay is essential. Your dog must be able to maintain his place regardless of where you are and what is going on around you. Stay is also the basis for many tricks and activities.

STATIONARY BEHAVIORS

The stationary behaviors are easiest to teach with luring. This will make the behavior happen quickly. Teddy will be highly motivated to perform, because he sees the reward directly under his nose or nearby. The key factor will be the placement of the lure. If your lure and visual cues *speak* to Teddy in an understandable way, he will respond immediately. Please study the photographs carefully; they show the *exact* placement of the lure for maximum effect.

Sit

Begin in a quiet room where there are few or no distractions. Prepare a pouch filled with treats so you don't have to pause during the session to get more. Place your clicker comfortably in the hand that will not be giving cues or treats.

1. Begin with targeting your hand. This tells your dog that it's time to play and he'll be all nose and attention on your hand.
2. Show your dog the treat by holding it between his eyes.
3. When he looks up, his rear end will automatically go down.
4. Click and reward.
5. Repeat this three times.
6. Now add the command, "Teddy, sit," as you lure him into position.
7. Do this three times.
8. Without luring your dog, say, "Teddy, sit."
9. If he does so, reward him. If not, use the lure again.

Hold the lure between the dog's eyes.

Teddy now knows how to sit on command. Test his knowledge by moving to a new place, just four feet from where you were working. Try again. If he performs as requested, click, praise, and reward. If not, he has not grasped the meaning of the verbal cue. Repeat the training sequence in the new place, then test Teddy again.

If your dog needs to be lured every time you move to a new location, it means he does not understand the meaning of the cue. Go back and reteach him the verbal cue in association with the luring action. Some dogs just need a little more repetition.

Now it's time to turn the lure into a visual cue. A very clear visual cue is your hand moving upward from the elbow, palm open, facing up. This cue is very similar to your initial arm movement when you were luring Teddy into the sit position.

Add the visual cue for sit.

1. Give Teddy the sit command as you present the visual cue close to him, just out of his reach.

2. He should sit on the verbal command, but will be watching your visual cue as well. Once he sits, click, praise, and reward.

3. Repeat at least three times.

4. Now try it with only the visual cue. Give the cue and wait.

5. If Teddy sits, click, praise, and reward.

6. If Teddy doesn't sit, return to using the verbal cue as well. He may need both the cues for a while before he can transfer to either alone.

Down

This particular position may be difficult for a dog with a dominant personality, but if you find a lure that is irresistible, he'll move into the down position as quickly as a less dominant dog would. Test the value of your treats and rewards before beginning this exercise. If you want absolute driven behavior, go for the ultimate value right from the start—steak!

1. Tell your dog to sit. (He should know this one by now.)

2. Place the lure under his nose and move it down until it is touching the floor. His head will follow the lure.

3. Click, praise, and reward.

4. Each time you do this, require more downward movement. While some dogs will automatically drop to the floor for the lure, others won't and you'll need to slowly shape the behavior.

5. The second Teddy's tummy touches the floor, click, praise, and reward.

While you want to maintain the requirement that down means tummy touching the floor, it's OK if Teddy rolls onto his side or back as he's learning the action. Later, you can shape the behavior to more sphinx-like positioning, if you wish. For now, the criterion is simply for the dog to lie down.

Once your dog can perform this action at least three times in a row, add the verbal cue for down as you lure Teddy into position. Your lure is working as a visual cue that Teddy will associate with the action of lying down. Use a distinct hand signal as you offer the lure. I always use my index finger pointing downward, because it is so different from the open hand gesture for stay.

As with sit, have Teddy perform the down in different locations. Slowly add distractions into the mix. A distraction can be the presence of a toy, or another family member, or simply working in another room. (See chapter 4 for more on distraction proofing.)

Mix up the exercises by alternating the sit and down commands.

The beginning of down . . .

. . . partway there . . .

. . . all the way down.

You may find that once you teach these behaviors, Teddy will be throwing them at you to obtain attention and rewards. Be sure not to offer any response unless you first requested the action. A mere word from you is enough reward for your dog to continue doing the behavior. While sitting and lying down for attention is far better than jumping on you, it is still a sign that the dog is pushing you into giving him what he wants, when he wants it. Giving your dog attention should always be your decision, not his.

Stand

This position can either be captured or lured. By capturing, I mean you simply click, praise, and reward when Teddy is standing still. Luring is a bit tougher, but it's less likely that Teddy will confuse his stand and bark, or stand and urinate, with only the stand command. Remember, whatever behavior you click your dog will repeat, because he knows that good things are coming. The timing of the click must be accurate to encourage the behavior you want.

1. If your dog is sitting and you want him to stand, place the lure just out of his reach on an even level with his nose.

2. As he reaches out for the lure, click, praise, and reward.

3. Request a little more movement forward each time before the click.

4. When Teddy is standing, click, praise, and give him several rewards. This is called jackpotting. When Teddy does the final exercise in full, he receives a jackpot of rewards.

5. Repeat this at least three times to make sure Teddy completely understands the exercise.

Reaching forward for the lure . . .

. . . into the stand.

Now it's time to add the verbal cue along with the visual cue you have already taught Teddy while luring him. Add the command "Teddy, stand," as you present the lure, always clicking, praising, and rewarding each success. After several repetitions, Teddy should connect the verbal cue with the action. Test this by using only the verbal cue. If Teddy doesn't stand, continue using the visual cue for a little longer. The stand can sometimes be difficult to do with only a verbal cue. Using the lure a little longer won't hurt his progress. It will only maintain his positive attitude and willingness to perform. Lures can be reduced later.

One way of making sure Teddy remains standing is to rub his tummy. Few dogs turn this down. He may start coming to you for a tummy rub and standing for this attention or throwing himself at your feet, tummy up. Whatever works!

MOVING BEHAVIORS

Moving behaviors can also be taught with either a lure or through capturing. Luring can make the behavior happen much faster, but should be phased out or it can become a crutch. Either way, the actions will require precise click and reward timing. You need to be aware of every minor accomplishment; reward it and stick to your criterion for the next level as you shape the behavior. The only reason to fall back is if Teddy gets lost at the next step, because this means the previous step wasn't clear. Sometimes you must regress to progress.

Heel

Luring into the heel position is the fastest and easiest way to teach this exercise, especially with puppies. Teddy already knows how to target. Now he must target in heel position—his shoulder even with your leg—and move with you. Begin with only a step or two and gradually add to that until you are able to walk with him through the house and yard.

1. The dog will heel on your left side, so place the lure in your left hand. That will be the target hand. (If you have a very small dog and can't easily bend over, you may want to use a target stick.) Hold the clicker in your right hand, with treats or toys in a pouch on your hip. A pouch will keep the treats easily accessible while keeping your hands free to target and click.

2. When Teddy comes to touch your target hand, click, praise, and reward.

3. Step forward two steps, starting out on your left leg (the leg closest to Teddy). When Teddy follows and touches the target, click, praise, and reward.

4. Each time Teddy accomplishes the task, add two or three steps. For example, begin with two steps, then take four steps, then six, and so on. Only move on if Teddy performs correctly. And remember, each level is rewarded with a click and treat.

Heel position with the lure at the dog's nose.

When you begin the heel, step forward on your left leg. This will be Teddy's visual cue.

5. When Teddy can move along at your side with you taking more than twenty steps, incorporate turns. Do a right turn, still targeting and luring Teddy around the turn. Stop, click, and reward. Then try a left turn.

If your dog lags or gets distracted, it means his threshold (how able he is or how long he can maintain his attention) has been breached. You'll need to go back a bit to a stage at which he was reliable. Let's say at twenty steps he starts becoming more interested in the birds flying overhead than in his target. Back up to heeling only fifteen steps between the click and the reward. Teddy may need more reinforcement at this level before moving on to the next.

Once Teddy has a good understanding of how to heel, it's time to use a leash. Hold the leash and the clicker in the same hand—the hand opposite your dog. The lure and target hand should be the hand closest to your dog (the left hand if Teddy is heeling on your left side).

Hold the leash loosely at all times; you don't want to drag your dog from place to place. A dog's natural reaction to a tight leash is to pull away, which means a tight leash will work against the learning process. You are starting this new exercise in a quiet, closed-in area, so there is no reason to use a training device such as a

Luring your dog around a right turn.

Just follow me . . .

. . . and we're there.

head halter. Attach the leash to a regular neck collar or body harness, preferably a Sense-sation or an Easy Walk harness. This gives you a little extra control but does not apply harsh punishment.

1. Begin with targeting. Put the lure in your left hand and the leash and clicker in your right hand.

2. Hold your right hand down near your right side or at your waist, never up in the air.

3. As you step forward on your left leg, tell your dog, "Teddy, heel."

Hold the leash and clicker in the same hand.

4. As with the training done without the leash, Teddy should be walking at your side, nose near the target, as you praise him. Click when your dog has reached the criteria you set for this exercise, stop, and give him his reward. *Don't* try to give him his reward while you walk. This will interrupt the flow of the exercise since he won't be paying attention while eating.

You may have noticed that I moved the praise from after the completion of the exercise to during the exercise. This encourages the dog to continue performing because it keeps his attention on you far better than if there were no vocal interaction at all. Without this interaction he will become easily distracted by anything around him that is more interesting than a treat held just out of his reach.

Teddy now knows that praise means a reward is on the way. He also knows that the sound of the click means a treat is imminent. Together, the sounds are rewarding both during his performance and at its completion. I have found that using praise in this way produces a happier performer, a dog who is rewarded by simply working for you. And this will help reduce your reliance on lures, treats, toys, and the clicker.

When the dog pulls ahead, redirect his attention by turning right.

During this stage of learning to walk on a loose leash, the leash is rarely if ever used. It is there merely to acclimate Teddy to its presence. If your dog moves in the wrong direction, it will enable you to refocus his attention on the lure by holding him near you as you put the lure directly under his nose, so you don't have to race after him and try to get him to pay attention again. Also keep in mind that if your dog tries to wander away, it means you have broken his threshold or advanced to a point where Teddy did not fully understand the exercise. The leash will help you get things back in order with less frustration.

When this happens, take break for a few minutes, then return to the stage where your dog was solid with the heel command without losing attention. Sometimes a little rest can help the brain work better. Begin again with either fewer steps or less time between the click and the reward.

As Teddy becomes consistent with his heeling, add the sit and other exercises. You can form a chain of behaviors before giving your dog the click and reward. For example, you can have him heel and sit, then click and treat; or heel, sit, and down, then click and treat. Another chain is to heel, stand, then sit and down. All of these chains can be done by reinforcing each step with praise, then click and reward when the chain is complete.

Come

The come, or recall, is one of the most important things for your dog to learn. It is imperative to have a dog who is reliable with this behavior. To accomplish this, Teddy must believe that coming to you is the most rewarding thing he could ever do. It's more rewarding than saying hello to other people or dogs. It's more rewarding than chasing a car or a squirrel. And it's more fun than swimming in the stinky, muddy pond and rolling in dead fish.

Benny was a 2-year-old Beagle with aggression issues. He refused to come when called, growled at his owner whenever he walked by, and would snap at people who woke him. Further, he pulled on the leash when walked and barked at those who passed.

One of the first things I noticed was how Benny was being touched. The owner would pat his sides. This is a very threatening gesture to a dog. Dogs prefer rubbing under the chin, on their chest, or on their belly. They don't like hard pats anymore than we do.

Once this handling issue was addressed, we taught Benny to come using a lure and reward. Being a chow hound (as many Beagles are) with a never-ending food drive, he learned quickly.

Benny now comes when he's called, and the other behaviors have been corrected through positive training techniques.

For Teddy to believe that you are the *ultimate* reward, you must prove it. This is done through a combination of luring, shaping, and capturing. You will use anything that works to get your dog's attention. The only thing you will never do is punish your dog when he comes to you. I have seen many dogs turned off the recall by having their owners call them to be punished. A punishment can be anything from being yelled at to physical abuse. I've even seen dogs who don't wish to go to their owners because of how the people touch them. The person can think they are showing affection, when the meaning to the dog is entirely different.

When working with a very young puppy, it's best to begin by luring. While pups prefer to be near pack members (you), they don't yet understand their environment, nor do they have any particular desire to please you. Praise doesn't have much meaning. When you begin pairing the food with the sound of the clicker and praise, they'll quickly make the connection.

Lure the dog to come to his target, your hand.

As with all new behaviors, start training in a quiet, enclosed area. This will ensure quick success.

1. Show your dog the treat. This begins the targeting exercise.

2. Click and praise, then give him the treat.

3. Repeat this at least three times.

4. Allow your dog to smell the treat, but hold it a short distance, say one foot away.

5. When your dog comes toward the treat, click and praise. Give him the treat when he gets to it.

6. Gradually increase the distance. Keep your target low so that your dog can see the visual cue of your hand holding the treat.

7. With each success, gradually increase the distance.

Click when the dog arrives in front of you. Eventually, you can add the sit.

8. As your dog becomes reliable, begin adding the verbal cue, "Teddy, come."

9. Gradually advance from making the click as Teddy begins toward you to clicking only when Teddy arrives.

10. When Teddy is reliably coming to you, with both the visual and the verbal cue, add another behavior, such as sit. This will eventually form an automatic chain of come and sit whenever your dog hears the come command. This is far better than having Teddy come and then leave again before you can gain control of him.

At this point you can begin involving other family members in a game with Teddy. A fun game is Round Robin. This will teach your dog to come and sit for everyone.

1. Begin with two people standing face to face, eight feet apart. Each person has treats and a clicker.

2. The person most familiar with training the dog is the first to call him.

3. When he arrives and sits, that person clicks and gives the reward.

4. After the reward is given, the next person calls Teddy to come and sit. Upon arrival, that person clicks and gives the reward.

5. Both people step back another foot or two and repeat the game.

Besides adding distance, you can also add more people. Anyone who can clearly tell your dog to come can participate. Make sure all participants are consistent with the cues and timing of the click and reward.

You can also add the Name Game. As each participant calls to Teddy, the person he is leaving tells him to go to that person ("Go to Elizabeth," for example). This adds new cues to Teddy's repertoire and further directs his behavior. The person he is going to should be praising him as he moves in the right direction. As he is rewarded upon arrival, he is reinforced for *listening* to the cues. Through repetition, the cues become meaningful.

Another game is the Out of Sight Recall. This is fun to play on a day when you can't go outside. You can do it yourself, but it is easier with two or more people. You and the other person hide in different parts of the house and take turns calling Teddy. As he learns the pattern, change your locations. This game is also useful for initiating a dog into search and rescue or assistance work. It teaches the dog to locate the origin of a sound as well as to listen to specific cues. If your goals are to compete in obedience or other performance trials, out of sight work is very valuable.

STAY

Teaching your dog to perform a solid, stationary stay will take time. It is one of the easiest behaviors to teach, unless Teddy is under five months of age—young pups have a difficult time remaining still. Building the stay in small increments will be important to overall success. As with all new commands, distraction proofing is also very important.

I break down the stay exercises into three parts:

1. Time. Regardless of the position, the dog needs to learn to remain in one place for more than a minute.
2. Movement. Teddy must remain in one place as he learns to accept you moving all the way around him.
3. Distance. As your dog learns to remain still despite your movement, gradually increase the distance as you did with the come exercises.

Time

We'll begin with the easiest stay position, sit-stay.

1. Tell your dog to sit. When he does, praise, click, and reward.
2. Repeat, but this time don't click until he has remained for a couple of seconds. I normally count the seconds by repeating out loud the phrase "good boy."
3. When you have reached two "good boys," praise, click, and reward.
4. Next time, ask him to remain through three "good boys," and so on, until you have reached at least six "good boys."

Now is the time to add the verbal and visual cues. The visual cue I use is clear and large: open palm facing the dog, fingers spread. The verbal cue is "stay," so as I tell my dog to stay, I also present him with my visual cue. He must remain in place for at least four "good boys," then I click and reward him. When first presenting the cues, I shorten the amount of time I require Teddy to stay before bridging (clicking) the command. This will ensure success. After several repetitions, Teddy will associate the cues with the action.

Make the stay signal clear and large.

1. Tell your dog to sit. Praise him as he does. But don't click yet.

2. As you step in front of your dog, face to face, tell him "stay." As he remains, say four "good boys." Click and reward. The reason I suggest standing in front of your dog is to reduce his tendency to move forward or toward you. Some dogs feel that being close to you will bring the reward faster. Remaining close in the beginning will reduce the dog's desire to move forward, thereby facilitating his success.

3. Go on to other moving exercises, such as heel, and other brief stationary positions. Mixing up the session will keep Teddy interested and offering behaviors for you. This is a happily working dog who wants to learn. Doing the same thing repeatedly will only bore you both.

4. The next time you work on sit-stay add one to two more "good boys."

5. With every three successful repetitions, ask him to stay for two to three more seconds before you click and treat.

Facing your dog during the sit-stay will keep him from wanting to wander toward you.

If your dog gets up during the stay, lure him back into position and go back to the amount of time he can stay successfully. Work at this level for a day or so before moving on to the next level.

When Teddy can remain in a sit-stay for more than a minute, you can begin adding minor distractions such as a toy nearby or someone else in the room, but nothing more distracting than that. As with all distractions, present them from a distance at which Teddy isn't bothered and gradually move them closer, a foot at a time. (Please read chapter 4 before you start working on distraction proofing.)

The main idea is to build upon successes. If you have to repeatedly return your dog to the sit-stay, it means he wasn't yet ready for that level. He doesn't understand what you want. Dogs aren't vindictive or bad. They really want to fit in with their family packs. Communication, patience, and repetition (CPR) will help them achieve this goal.

I've worked with many Golden Retrievers who find that being touched is a far better reward than food treats. Once they understand that they will be touched while they remain in a stay, you have a Golden statue. However, it's tough to reduce the touch before I start moving around, so I tend to touch some part of them while I move. It can be a light touch on the head or under the chin. The dog is just thrilled to feel you. This also works well for dogs who are very attached to their people or have severe separation anxiety.

Once you and Teddy are proficient with the sit-stay, try adding the stay to the down and stand exercises. You may find that while your dog can perform a down-stay very easily, he has some trouble with the stand-stay. The reason is that he can't easily move out of a down, but stepping forward is natural while standing. I find that rubbing the dog's tummy during the exercise rewards the dog enough to convince him to remain in position as long as you wish. In fact, with some dogs it can be more rewarding than clicking and treating. Of course, you must fade out this reward before you start moving during the stays.

Adding Movement

The next step in building a solid stay is to move around and away from the dog. As with all exercises, you need to work in incremental steps. With movement, I present it to the dog like this.

Stroking Teddy's tummy during the stand-stay will encourage him to remain still.

Use a clear signal for the down-stay.

1. Stepping side to side in front of the dog.
2. Moving along his sides, near his shoulder.
3. Moving along his sides, near his ribs.
4. Moving along his sides, near his hips.
5. Moving completely around him once.
6. Moving completely around him once in each direction.
7. Moving completely around him twice in each direction.

You may or may not have to further break down the movement. It depends on your dog. While some may need just a few tries to get comfortable with your walking around them, others may require a couple of training sessions. As with any new task, work at your dog's pace. If he begins breaking his stay, go back to his comfort zone for a while. And be sure to practice this and other exercises both on and off the leash.

If you are using a target stick (rather than having your dog target your hand), be sure to keep the stick stationary (that is, pointing at the same spot) while you are moving around your dog, since, if it moves, so does Teddy.

Moving along the dog's side, near his shoulder, during a sit-stay.

Moving along the dog's side, near his hips, during a sit-stay.

Using the target stick during the down-stay.

As I walk around Teddy during the sit-stay, the target stick will remain at his nose.

It's not difficult to walk around your dog during the stand-stay while keeping the target stick stationary.

When you start to move around your dog in the down-stay or stand-stay, I suggest you first move back along his side. Once the dog can handle this, go behind him, then back to his side. As he accepts these motions, continue to his other side and finally all the way around. For the dog who tends to move as you stand upright, concentrate on that motion before moving along his sides. Different dogs require a different series of steps to shape behaviors. As with humans, dogs are all individuals. So you'll need to adjust your training to suit your dog.

Distance

Now that Teddy accepts staying in one spot for more than a minute with you moving completely around him, you can add the distance factor. This, as with all other criteria, must be done incrementally—one foot at a time. Praise Teddy the entire time he remains in position and with each success, click and reward.

Gaining distance on a down-stay.

Gaining distance on a sit-stay.

Gaining distance on a stand-stay.

If he moves, use the verbal correction "no!" and then lure him back into place. If this happens more than once or twice, back up to the distance where Teddy didn't move and work on that for a while. Add the down, stand, and heel to keep your sessions interesting.

When Teddy is comfortable performing the sit-stay indoors or within a quiet, enclosed area, it's time to go outdoors and face the reality of distractions. As always, have Teddy on a leash. If he is prone to reacting to distractions, also use a training device.

If you're using a harness and need to correct your dog for leaving the stay position, use the leash to bring him back to the location, then lure him with your visual cue, then tell Teddy to stay. With a head halter, guide Teddy back to the same position with the leash, then use a gentle forward and upward motion under his chin to replace him in the sit position. (If you're doing a stand-stay, don't use the leash further after returning him to the spot.) If you're doing a down-stay, don't pull downward. First try to lure Teddy into position with the treat. Once he's down, repeat the stay command.

If Teddy will not respond to the lure, you will need to place him into position, because you can't allow him to ignore your command. This would teach him that your words are not meaningful. To place Teddy into the down position, hold the entire leash in your left hand. Hold both front legs with your right hand. Press down *gently* on the shoulders with your left hand as you bring his front legs forward. Praise and reward the moment he reaches the correct position—even though you did the work. Since your hands are filled with Teddy, you may not be able to click.

Placing the dog in the down position.

As you and your dog complete the exercises in this chapter, you will become proficient with all the basic commands. These include walking on a loose leash (heel), sit-stay, down-stay, come, and stand-stay. Each of these will be used in some manner throughout the remainder of this book and in your everyday lives. Practicing these exercises every day, during all kinds of ordinary activities, will give your dog the repetition he needs to fully understand and respond to your commands at all times. Moreover, he'll most likely be throwing them at you whenever he wants attention. This is one of the side effects of clicker training.

If your dog is constantly trying to get your attention by throwing behaviors at you, it means he has been getting rewarded for doing so. Unless you intend to always wear a clicker and give him rewards, only offer the click when you request the behavior. At first, Teddy will increase his random behaviors, but when he sees that it doesn't earn him anything, he'll eventually give it up.

All training must be positive, but still on your terms, with you making the decisions.

Chapter 4

Just Do It!

Once Teddy is working nicely both inside and outside in a quiet area, it's time to begin adding distractions. All distractions are different, and dogs experience them in different ways. A toy may not be as difficult to ignore as another animal—unless your dog happens to have a very strong interest in toys. The distraction of other people may be even more difficult to deal with than toys or other animals. How distracting something is always depends upon your dog.

You should always begin distraction proofing with the thing that is least distracting to your dog. Let's suppose Teddy is least distracted by toys and most distracted by another dog. In that case, you break down the presentation of distractions as follows:

1. Toys
2. People
3. New places
4. One dog
5. More than one dog

If Teddy is most distracted by people, you would put that at the end of the list. If going to a new place is more of a distraction than other dogs, that's the last thing presented. In other words, all distraction proofing should be done from the least distracting to the most distracting. Initially, the distraction should begin far enough away from your dog that it does not take his attention away from his desire to perform.

With each distraction, you shape Teddy's behavior as follows.

1. Work with your dog at a *safe* distance from the distraction; that is, the distance at which he takes no notice of the distraction.

2. As Teddy consistently works well, taking no notice of the distraction, place the distraction a foot closer.

3. Gradually increase the proximity of the distraction in one-foot increments as Teddy consistently performs as requested. When Teddy takes notice of the distraction and decides he'd rather have that item than pay attention, back up to a distance where he was performing well.

If an item is particularly distracting, you can also use it as Teddy's reward. His attention means it is more valuable to him than the reward you are offering. Granted, this can only be done if the item is a stick, a toy, or food. Obviously, you can't hold another dog or squirrel (or even another person) and use it as a lure for targeting. But you can allow Teddy to play with the other dog or person as an ultimate reward when the training session is completed (squirrel chasing is not

---

Many dogs I have worked with have had huge toy drives. I once worked with a German Shepherd who loved the tennis ball. Currently I'm working with a Labrador Retriever who loves an oddly shaped squeaky toy. These dogs prefer playing with their toy and will tune out everything else around them. While the initial basic obedience training took a little longer, the distraction proofing was almost immediate—provided the dog knew I held the toy.

The toy was initially used as a lure, and finally as a reward. As the dogs learned the behavior that earned them the click and reward of receiving their toy, they

began demonstrating other behaviors in the hope of receiving the toy. (Allowing the dog to mouth the toy was a minor reward, while throwing it for him was a major reward—the jackpot!)

It's interesting to note that both these dogs suffered from separation anxiety. They did not obsess about the toy solely as a play object, but also as a security blanket—a constant in their lives. Watching their people interacting with the toy further promoted the bond between owner and dog. The entire process of learning to respond to commands by getting their toy as a reward reduced their anxieties and helped these dogs relax.

Using a toy as a lure.

recommended). Using the higher value reward will keep his attention on you and will reduce the chances of something else distracting him.

As you increase the distraction factor, you will need to decrease the time you expect Teddy to perform. For example, if Teddy can heel for twenty steps, then do a sit and down without distractions, then when you add distractions, lower the requirements to a ten-step heel and a sit before the click and reward. As he improves his performances, add more steps to the heel and ask for other stationary positions. Backing up to *very easy* tasks when your dog is first presented with distractions will maintain his positive attitude, as well as yours.

USING A TRAINING DEVICE

As you move from easy distractions to more difficult ones, you might want to begin using a training device. For a dog who merely looks at a distraction and doesn't lunge toward it, a Sense-sation harness might work very well. However, if your dog does lunge after the distraction (and many will go after another dog or animal), I recommend using a head halter. It's better to guide your dog's head than pull on his neck. (While the Sense-sation harness is great for a dog who pulls only a little, it will not control a dog who is adamant about going after something.)

Once Teddy is watching you, you can often regain his attention with the lure. If not, back off on the distraction again until Teddy is working with you instead of showing more interest in the distraction. Of course, many real-life situations don't allow you to back off to a safety zone. When you're walking down the street or into the veterinarian's office, you will need a way of controlling your dog. When they're distracted, many dogs won't care about food or toy rewards, because it is more rewarding to go after the other animals. In these situations you can't allow your dog this particular reward. A training device will give you the necessary control.

I will discuss the two devices I use the most: the Sense-sation harness and the head halter. As I have already mentioned, I no longer use choke chains or prong collars. I rarely use a martingale collar, even for dogs who pull or are easily distracted, because it can lead to the same tracheal damage as any neck collar. This is a book on clicker training, which uses positive reinforcement (offering something the dog likes to reward good behavior), and a device that uses pain to teach has no place here.

That said, although clicker training is a positive way of teaching, it is not an end in and of itself. Few dogs can learn with purely positive reinforcement. There must be a balance. That is nature; that is life.

Using a humane training device along with the clicker will offer a way of correcting the dog without causing mental or physical damage. As the dog learns that he must pay attention, regardless of the circumstances, the training device can be used less and less, until eventually it is no longer necessary.

Distraction Proofing with a Sense-sation Harness

The Sense-sation harness has three straps: one has a ring in the middle and goes around the dog's chest, and the other two connect around the dog's girth. The leash attaches to the ring in the center of the dog's chest. By pulling at the center of the dog's gravity, you can control where his body moves. The pulling does not inflict any pain or discomfort. It merely guides your dog in the direction you want him to go.

If you're heeling and Teddy decides to go toward another dog, and no amount of food or toys can deter him, pull straight forward from his chest so that the leash is level with the chest. Then make a turn, and pull the leash into the turn with you. As Teddy regains his interest in you, click and reward.

Let's suppose Teddy will not comply with your sit and stay commands. Pulling upward on the leash will slightly lift his weight off his front end and settle it in his rear, making his rear end drop. The moment his rear is in the spot you wish, praise and release the leash tension. If this is all you requested, then click and reward. However, if you also wanted Teddy to stay, give the stay cues again and click when that exercise has been completed. I do suggest that you reduce your criteria a bit at this time, as Teddy has reached his threshold in this particular environment. You need to regress a bit to return to positive training.

The start position for heel with the Sense-sation harness.

Correct your dog for forging ahead by pulling the leash into a turn with you.

If your dog does not lie down on command or gets up out of a down-stay, you cannot do much of a correction with the harness. You will need to first try luring him. If this doesn't work, place Teddy into position. Reiterate the stay command, but shorten the time you ask him to stay. Click and reward when he accomplishes your request.

It's inevitable that there will be times when you have to regress a bit due to a distraction, but don't believe for a moment that you are going backward in your training. Distractions present an entirely new dimension, and you will need to retreat to a point in Teddy's training where everything is easy. When your dog regains reliability, you can once again present the distractions. This time, though, you might want to

Correct for not sitting or leaving a sit-stay by pulling up on the leash.

further break down the increments so that he is better able to manage them. A time will come when Teddy will respond no matter what is going on around him.

Distraction proofing is most difficult in a group training situation. During the first couple of lessons most dogs only want to play with one another, not learn obedience. When they are first introduced to group training, many dogs don't care about food or toy lures. They are far more rewarded by interaction with the other dogs. Their owners spend more time trying to hold them in check than actually learning anything. This can be frustrating for everyone involved.

For many years I refused to teach group lessons unless the dogs involved had previously worked with me individually and had been started on distraction proofing. The group class was then merely an extension of the distraction proofing.

Now that I have once again begun to offer beginner group classes, I am happy with more minor accomplishments. The fact that a dog can learn to sit on command in a group setting is a great accomplishment. If the dog can learn to walk on a leash, that's a miracle! However, the dog's success relies totally on the owner's patience, diligence (that is, practice), and consistency. Play with other dogs can be used as a jackpot reward, but you must first be able to control the dog within a group environment. Training devices, such as a head halter, are highly effective in these settings.

Although a group setting is less expensive, I'd highly recommend attending some individual classes first. They set Teddy up for success.

DISTRACTION PROOFING WITH A HEAD HALTER

Before entering any high-stress situation, make sure Teddy is totally comfortable wearing a head halter. Many dogs will rub against their handler or the ground when a halter is put on. Others will paw at their face. Once training has begun, this behavior fades away.

Think of a head halter as a new hat. At first it's itchy. After awhile you don't really know it's there anymore. If Teddy is doing back flips, however, take the halter off and try another brand. If he's still doing back flips, go to the Sense-sation or Easy Walk harness. Some dogs simply can't work with a head halter. Causing stress is not a great way to begin a positive training experience.

Always put the device on using targeting until Teddy learns to put his nose through himself. This is a dog who understands that the fun begins when the head halter is on and not before. Positive associations lead to positive results.

Here's how you put a head halter on your dog.

1. Practice the targeting on your hand with sit-stay a couple of times. Always click and reward as Teddy responds correctly.

2. Hold your target through the nosepiece of the head halter.

3. Once the dog puts his nose through, click and reward. (If your hands are full, enlist the aid of someone else to click or simply praise enthusiastically.)

4. As Teddy is eating his treat or holding his toy, buckle the back strap tight enough to barely fit two fingers between the strap and Teddy's neck. This allows for a snug fit without cutting off circulation or causing discomfort.

5. As soon as the head halter is on, begin the training session. Begin with exercises that Teddy thoroughly understands and enjoys. This will quickly take his mind off the fact that he is wearing something new.

Don't require the same high level of performance when you first put the head halter on. For example, if Teddy was heeling with you for forty steps and performing

Use the lure to get Teddy to target through the nosepiece of the head halter.

Reward him when his nose is through.

sit-stays for a minute with you walking around him, regress to ten steps and a brief sit-stay.

Some dogs are so distracted by the head halter that you'll need to regress to a mere two or three steps of heeling before you click and reward. Since Teddy is already familiar with the exercise, the progression will be quick, but you'll still need to return to constant rewards and possibly even luring before the reward. When your dog is once again on track, you can dispense with the lure and just click and reward. Lures need to be diminished, but rewards should always be available. We all need to get paid for our work. Teddy is no different.

A conventional head halter should fit this way at the back of your dog's neck.

When heeling with a head halter, if your dog forges ahead or moves away from you, pull downward and then turn in the opposite direction from whatever has caught his attention. The moment he is back at your side watching you, tell him sit, then click and reward. Decrease the number of steps you take in the heel position until you regain the majority of Teddy's attention. The fact that he was distracted enough to pull away means his threshold was breached.

Heeling with a head halter.

Always use the head halter with a loose leash. This is essential. A tight leash will be constantly applying pressure to your dog's nose, which means punishment at all times. A head halter correction should be very brief, with a light pressure on the nose. Once the dog is back in the correct position, the pressure is gone and the dog is praised. Remember that your constant, happy praise will do more to maintain Teddy's attention than a tight leash and lots of punishment. Your neighbors might think you're a little nutty, but they will appreciate your efforts when your dog is a well-behaved neighbor.

There may be some situations in which you'll need to use the head halter to correct Teddy for leaving the stay. When working with a distraction, you can count

If your dog moves away from you, pull downward and turn away from the distraction.

on this happening. Here's how to correct for getting up from a sit or a sit-stay. (This is also the correction for aggression.)

1. The moment Teddy breaks the command, use your verbal correction, "no."
2. Bring Teddy back to his original position using the leash.
3. Tell him "sit." Click and reward if he does. If not, gently pull forward (with the leash) and upward under his chin as you put light pressure on his hind end.
4. The moment Teddy is back in position, loosen the leash, then click and reward. If you have been working on stay as well, repeat the stay cues, wait a few moments (approximately the same amount of time he had stayed before getting up), praise, then click and reward.
5. Gradually increase the stay time with each successive repeat of this exercise. Keep in mind, however, that you'll need to decrease the time and/or movement with each increase of distraction.

When using the head halter to correct your dog for leaving the down position, you should *not* pull downward. First, try luring him back into position. If the lure doesn't work, you can either wait for the action to occur (and a properly clicker-trained dog will throw this out at you), or place the dog into position as described in chapter 3. (The exception is when you are working with an aggressive or very dominant dog who might bite while being placed into position. I'll discuss those dogs in chapter 8.) When they are distracted, the very best clicker-trained dogs might forget the things they've learned, and a little reminder might be in order.

When correcting a dog for not coming when called, always first try luring to regain your dog's attention. If this does not work, step backward as you give the verbal correction, and give the leash a little pull as you step back. This will *remind* Teddy that you're still present and wanting his attention. Walking backward a few steps can also refocus his attention on you because movement helps attract the dog's eye. After all, it was probably movement of some sort that took his attention away in the first place.

Gently pull forward and upward to correct your dog for leaving the sit.

Because you are almost reteaching the recall when you start adding distractions, return to calling your dog to you from a shorter distance. Your closer proximity makes it easier for Teddy to comply. If he still stares in the direction of the distraction, put yourself between him and the distraction if you can. This ensures that he'll come to you, because that's the direction he wants to go. Once he arrives, you click. And guess what? Teddy will return his attention to you for his reward. Do a few more of these exercises, then try to have your dog come to you from a direction just slightly different from the distraction.

Throughout the training process you need to remain flexible. Nothing is written in stone. Dog training requires imagination and patience. Every living thing responds differently to different situations. Work with your dog, not against him. A positive experience will translate into great results.

PHASING OUT TRAINING TOOLS

Eventually you want to have clear communication with your dog without the assistance of training tools. That is the goal of nearly everyone who trains their dog. They dream of having the dog comply with their requests, regardless of distractions and without any collar or leash.

Think it's impossible? Never. I don't care what the breed or age of the dog. It can be done. You started training off leash, so why not finish off leash?

When you began training in a quiet area with no training device or leash attachment, you had Teddy's total attention because there wasn't anything to distract him. As you introduced Teddy to new places, events, and environments, his attention suddenly went out the window. Some dogs couldn't care less about a click sound and the promise of treats or toys when a distraction is more inviting.

Distraction proofing can take quite a bit of time; often longer than the initial training of all the commands. Patience and persistence will get you there. While some dogs can work in any environment in a matter of weeks, others take years. Don't give up!

The clearest signal that it's time to reduce the use of a training device is when you rarely, if ever, need to use it. Some dog owners will continue using the harness or head halter as insurance. I believe it's a crutch; no training tool is forever.

My two dogs watch me.

Your communication, through verbal and visual cues, is all a well-trained dog needs.

When I take my dogs for a walk in the woods or to perform at shows, they only wear their decorative neck collars that hold their tags. The collars aren't used for correction. If I'm in an area where there's a leash law, I attach a leash but rarely use it. I always use my verbal and visual cues. If something grabs my dog's attention, I use the low, growly tone to focus them back on me. I reward with praise when I see their eyes. In fact, I have more than one dog, and both listen simultaneously.

When Teddy is at the point where he's not paying much attention to distractions of any sort, test his attentiveness by making unexpected turns, and changing your pace and the order of the exercises. If he is responding quickly and precisely, it's time to reduce the use of the training device. If not, work a little longer.

Phasing Out the Leash

To have control at a distance, Teddy must know that you don't really need a leash to communicate with or correct, him. Work on phasing out the leash will further strengthen your communication, enabling you to dispense with both the leash and, eventually, any other training device or tool.

The first exercise to accomplish will be the finish. This is an exercise that puts your dog into heel position from anywhere. There are two forms of the finish: going around the handler's back and into position; and moving to the handler's side and into position. The type of finish your dog will do best depends largely on the dog, but many can do both. If you want your dog to do both, be sure to distinguish the two exercises by using very different visual and verbal cues.

Finish Around Your Back

This is a finish to the right, and it assumes Teddy is heeling on your left side. While you can always use the clicker to simply mark the moment that Teddy is in heel position, it is not easy to shape him into going around for the finish. For this I use a lure. The click is earned at the completion of the exercise, to mark the moment Teddy is in the finish position.

1. Get Teddy into training mode by doing some exercises that are fun and easy.

2. Stand facing Teddy.

3. Place half the leash, along with a lure, in your right hand. The other half of the leash should be slack. Show Teddy the lure to get his attention on your target hand.

4. As you tell Teddy to heel, step back on your right leg and bring your right arm back along with your leg. Teddy already knows the meaning of heel, so he will follow the movement of your right leg. The target is just extra incentive.

Preparing for a finish to the right, around the handler's back.

5. As he moves back along your leg, praise, but don't click or treat yet.

6. Bring your right leg forward and transfer the leash and lure, behind your back, from your right hand to your left.

7. Lure Teddy to your left side.

8. When his head is even with your left heel, say, "Teddy, sit." I tell the dog to sit before he reaches the proper heel position because it takes a few seconds for him to actually sit down. If you are blessed with a dog who responds as fast as you speak, wait a little longer before giving the sit command.

Step back on your right leg, moving your right arm at the same time. Teddy is targeting your right hand.

9. When Teddy sits, click and reward. If Teddy overshoots the proper position, don't click. Just do the exercise again. The click signifies the end of the exercise. If you must do the exercise again, you must not signal the end by clicking. You can, however, praise Teddy as he performs any portion of the exercise correctly. Praise is a way of encouraging your dog to keep going.

Preparing for finish to the left, along your side.

Finish to the Left

You have already taught Teddy to assume the heel position upon command, so this finish to the left will be very natural for him. Few dogs will naturally go the long way around, and the finish behind your back *is* the long way around.

There are two ways you can do this exercise. The first is simply to tell Teddy to heel. He should place himself in position. Using shaping, you can attain the exact position you want. The second way is to lure him into position this way.

1. Stand facing your dog.
2. Place half of the leash in your left hand and leave the other half slack.
3. Put the lure in your left hand.
4. As you tell Teddy to heel (or use the command Swing if you are teaching Teddy to finish in both directions), step back on your left leg. Move your left arm, which the dog is targeting, along with your leg.
5. As the dog moves along your leg, bring the leash out away from your body so he must step out a bit.
6. When Teddy is even with your left leg (the one that stepped back), bring the leg forward as you bring the leash close to your left side.
7. As your dog moves along your side, tell him "sit."

Phasing Out the Sense-sation or Easy Walk Harness

It's very easy to reduce the use of a harness. It wasn't much of a training device to begin with—more of a *reminder* to pay attention. You began by attaching the leash to both the collar and harness; now, go back to that step, as shown in the photo on page 68. If you're adept at using both hands, you can also put one leash

Begin the finish by showing
your dog the lure.

As you tell Teddy to heel,
step back with your left leg.

Bring the leash out and
away from your body, so
Teddy must step out.

Bring your leg forward as
you move the leash close
to your left side.

As your dog moves along
your side . . .

. . . give him the sit
command.

The leash is attached to both the collar and the harness.

on the harness and another on the dog's collar.

If Teddy is heeling on your left, the leash attached to his collar should be held in your left hand. Keep the leash that's attached to the harness in your right hand as a backup. Hold the clicker in your right hand as well. (Be careful not to press it if you need to correct your dog with that hand.)

Go through your normal training routines. Use your right hand to apply any training corrections; otherwise both leashes should remain loose and you should use your verbal and visual cues before *any* use of the leash. Say, for example, that you are walking along. Teddy becomes distracted by a cat grooming herself on the front lawn of a nearby house. When you see him look in the direction of the cat, use a low, growly "no," give the harness a tug, and turn in the opposite direction. When Teddy looks at you, stop, click, and reward. If Teddy returns his attention to you before you have to make the turn, stop, click, and reward him for that. The sooner your dog returns his attention to you, the sooner he hears his click.

If you are working on a stay exercise and you see Teddy's attention wander, use your low, growly "no." The second he looks at you, click and reward. Keep in mind that if you praise him the entire time Teddy is behaving properly, he'll be less likely to become distracted because he knows good things are coming.

Concentrate on your activity with your dog, not on what is happening around you. If you don't react to a distraction, Teddy is also less likely to react. Your dog takes his cues from you, his pack leader.

Phasing Out the Head Halter

Many dog trainers and dog owners are tempted to use a head halter every day throughout their dog's life. It seems like a miracle tool that offers great control in all situations. However, the head halter is merely a training tool and should be phased out—as should any tool.

While it can often be used when you're walking your dog through the neighborhood, there are many situations in which it can't be used. Moreover, unenlightened passersby will still think the halter is a muzzle and that your dog is aggressive.

The bottom line is that you need to have complete communication with Teddy, regardless of whether he is wearing the head halter. There will be times when this control can save his life. Death and injury statistics are very high for dogs who

Using a head halter that doesn't apply pressure when it is not in use is the best way to acclimate your dog to not needing one at all. Remember that the conventional head halter (the one that looks like a horse halter) offers no pressure unless it is applied. Using this type of head halter will be easier to phase out than the figure-8 head halter. The conventional head halter may be present, but it is not giving constant punishment. A figure-8 head halter, due to its design, does cause constant pressure (unless you have the noseband very loose), so it will be more difficult to phase out. Keep in mind, however, that the mere presence of any head halter will cause a dog to behave better, because he has learned that you have better control whenever the halter is present.

rush through the front door or an open gate and into a busy road. A dog who will stop running and come when called is far safer. You simply can't leave a training device on Teddy all the time.

I normally phase out the head halter while working on long-distance training. However, you can start the process at the same time you're phasing out the leash. You will rarely need to use the pressure of a head halter while you are reducing the use of the leash, because Teddy should be paying attention to figure out how fast you are walking and which way you might turn. You'll have a dog who is watching your every move and doesn't need any reminders.

Let's say your dog pays attention 95 percent of the time. There may be a few situations in which you need to do a leash correction, but they will be rare. You can work on leash reduction techniques by beginning to drop the noseband on the head halter if you are sure you will not encounter the specific situation that distracts Teddy. If you are in a distracting situation, use the noseband on the halter; otherwise, you are setting yourself up for failure and possibly causing your dog to regress.

A dog who is attentive is a dog who doesn't need leash corrections of any sort. He might be wearing the head halter, but you won't be using it. If you find you are using it more than a couple times during a training session, it means Teddy isn't yet ready for off-leash work, nor for you to reduce the use of the head halter.

Clicker training and positive techniques only work when you can set your dog up for, and build upon, success.

The head halter is reduced by *faking out your dog*. He still has it on, but the nose strap is no longer in place. I begin by pulling off the noseband during the stay

A head halter with the noseband off.

When you started clicker training, you began by rewarding Teddy each time he performed correctly. This was necessary to teach him new things. Now that Teddy knows the exercises you are working on, you need to vary his reward schedule so that you can obtain a better performance.

If he doesn't receive a reward for sitting crookedly and does when he sits straight, he will strive to sit straight. If he only receives a reward for heeling close to your leg and not for merely meandering in the vicinity of your leg, he will strive to heel closer. The better Teddy performs, the more you should expect from him. This makes him constantly strive to do better, because he knows it earns him his click and reward.

and come exercises. Teddy is less likely to commit an error during these exercises, so there'll be less need for any leash correction.

1. Put Teddy in a sit-stay or down-stay.
2. Pull down the noseband on the head halter.
3. Walk around him in both directions. Praise him as he remains.
4. Return to his side, then click and reward.
5. Repeat this exercise throughout the training session.

An alternate exercise is to have Teddy come to you, then sit. When he sits, click and reward.

When you need to put the noseband back into place, lure his nose through with the target, or take the head halter off and put it on again. Click and reward when it is back on his nose. You don't want Teddy thinking that you are punishing him when you replace the noseband before the heel.

To phase out the head halter while heeling, attach one leash to the collar and the other to the head halter.

To phase out the head halter while heeling, I suggest using two leashes (or one leash with a clip on each side). One should be attached to Teddy's regular collar, the other to the head halter. Place the leash that is attached to his collar in your right hand, and the leash attached to the head halter in your left hand.

As always, both leashes should be loose; don't use them unless it's absolutely necessary. Always praise as Teddy remains in the proper place. When he is performing exceptionally well, stop, click, and praise. Vary the amount of time between this bridging so that your dog doesn't pick up on any specific pattern to his rewards. This variable reward schedule will produce a more attentive dog.

While walking with the double leashes, continually praise Teddy as he pays attention. If he becomes distracted, say "no" in the low, growly tone and use the head halter leash as a correction. By now Teddy might just correct himself when you growl "no." If he does, immediately stop, click, and reward. If he doesn't, keep moving until he is in the appropriate place, then stop, click, and reward.

When you find that you almost never have to use the leash attached to the head halter, drop the noseband on the head halter while you work.

As Teddy performs without you having to use either leash, take off the head halter.

You and Teddy now have complete communication with no need for a training device.

Chapter 5

Click to Behave

Clicker training isn't limited to basic obedience or to dogs of any particular age. Because the clicker is so effective for marking the moment when Teddy has done something right, it can be a quick way to teach housetraining and to help correct bad habits—or, in the case of puppies, prevent bad habits. This type of training can also teach dogs to redirect their attention from bad behaviors, such as barking and digging, to something that is more positive.

What we consider to be bad behaviors are often merely natural behaviors, instinctive to every dog. Such behaviors can often be a result of boredom and/or anxiety, but they are not expressions of anger or spite. The good news is that for every "bad" behavior there is an alternate, acceptable behavior. It is your job to redirect Teddy to the acceptable behavior using the clicker and positive training techniques.

As with distraction proofing, there might not be a purely positive way of correcting all inappropriate behavior. You may have to punish your dog from time to time. Punishment can range from a simple "no" to ostracizing him from the family pack. You should *never* resort to yelling or hitting, regardless of your own frustration level. Some dogs will become very aggressive as a result, while others might develop terrible anxiety. All corrections must be done in a way that Teddy understands, using canine language. Dogs correct one another through growling, snapping, body pushing, and ostracism; you will use your growly "no" and ostracism—leave the snapping and pushing to the canines.

The main idea of behavior modification with a clicker is to redirect Teddy to the behavior you want, then click and reward when he does the right thing. Depending on the behavior, this can take minutes or months. For complete success, you must use CPR (consistency, patience, and repetition) throughout the process. Giving up in exasperation is not an option. You must also realize that

I always teach my dogs to keep off the furniture, not to jump up, not to counter surf or chew on shoes, and not to carry their stainless steel dishes around the house or drop them on the ceramic tile floor. But when we are working on filming television commercials, the dog is often required to do these very behaviors. Telling the writers that this promotes bad behavior is not an option. Instead, I must shape the behavior and make sure it is performed *only* on cue and not on whim.

There are times shortly after filming one of these commercials that one of my dogs tries to do the behavior he has been taught for the camera, and I have to correct him because I did not give him the cue.

I cannot attribute the action to them throwing out behaviors in an attempt to earn a treat. That's because these kinds of behaviors are self-satisfying actions for the dog. The reward of getting on the sofa (being on a comfortable, centrally located "bed") is enough all by itself. So is the reward of my reaction (hands to my ears, wrinkled brow, and a loud "yikes!") to the loud clang of the dog dish on the tile floor. Who says dogs don't have a sense of humor? I've known many who do.

dogs don't understand gray areas such as "sometimes," "maybe," "it's okay this time but not next time," and "you can do it if . . ." Dogs understand the all-or-nothing rule: They can either do it all the time or none of the time.

After Teddy has learned how this rule relates to each specific behavior (it's an allowed behavior or it's not), you can teach him a specific cue that allows him to do something he was taught not to do. However, he may be reluctant about performing if it entails something he has already learned *not* to do. Why confuse him?

HOUSETRAINING

Regardless of the method you use to housetrain your puppy, success is based on CPR. You must be very observant and frequently take your dog to the area you have designated for him to relieve himself. The younger the dog, the more often he has to relieve himself. Puppies have faster metabolisms than older dogs, and less ability to control their bodies. This, coupled with their high activity level, means they must eliminate more often. The more active the pup, the more often he will have to go. There are also some other sure-fire potty moments: when the dog wakes up, within fifteen to twenty minutes after eating, after training, and when he's stressed.

Some pups will urinate when they are excited. This is called submissive urination. You should never correct Teddy when this happens, because he has no control over this behavior. The best way of handling this situation is to avoid overexcited moments when you're indoors. Have Teddy greet people outside the door. Or have people ignore him inside until he settles a bit. You can be assured

Once a dog has an understanding of where to relieve himself, he will try to tell you when he needs to go there. He might sit at the door and whine. Or he might circle and sniff. Another cue is when he sits and stares at you. When your dog is trying to initiate a game, most commonly he'll lower his front end and raise his back end in what is called a play bow. When he needs to go outdoors to relieve himself, he will sit and stare or show overall restlessness. Remember, though, that each dog is different; yours may show one or more of these signals, or a signal all his own. Through observation, you will learn to understand your dog's cues.

that unless there is a physical ailment causing the condition, your puppy will eventually outgrow the problem.

When you cannot observe Teddy, place him in a secure place where he has no access to areas you do not wish him to mess. A crate or an exercise pen is ideal. Dogs instinctively keep their dens clean. Because the crate simulates the environment of a den, Teddy will likely learn to contain himself until he is let outdoors to his relief area. For those dogs who do not have this innate desire (puppies who have spent some time in a pet shop window are one example), housetraining can be more difficult—but not impossible.

It helps to have an adult dog who is already well versed in housetraining procedures. Many pups will follow the lead of another dog. They see the other dog relieve himself in a particular spot and will do the same. They will especially pick up on this if the other dog is rewarded for doing so; dogs seek rewarding behavior.

Try to keep a schedule—a list of times when Teddy will be taken to his relief area. Dogs are creatures of habit. Once they learn a regular schedule, it is easier for them to adjust themselves. Teddy will know when and where he will be rewarded for relieving himself and will learn faster. Most dogs with housetraining issues have never been given a chance to learn this, nor have they the necessary constant observation and supervision.

When you have a puppy, you need to approach the situation as if you were watching over a human toddler. The toddler is never left alone, unless she is sleeping safely in a crib. Otherwise, she is always observed, specific behavioral clues are noted, and she is kept out of danger. Most parents have been through this. Noticing the child's specific behaviors helps with potty training, expediting the overall process. The more attention they give the situation, the faster the toddler graduates from diapers.

Let's begin with a simple schedule, one that can be maintained or slightly modified depending on your work routine. We will also assume that little Teddy will be crated or penned while he is sleeping at night and when you are unable to observe him. Keep in mind that a dog should never be crated both day and night for long periods of time. This causes many problems, both physical and mental.

Limit Teddy's crate time to no more than five to six hours during the night and a couple of hours at a stretch during the day.

6 a.m.	Take Teddy to his relief area.
7 a.m.	Take Teddy to his relief area. Bring him inside and feed him. Let him out again within twenty minutes.
9 a.m.	Take Teddy to his relief area.
11 a.m.	Take Teddy to his relief area.
12 p.m.	Feed Teddy if he is under 5 months of age. Let him out within twenty minutes.
2 p.m.	Take Teddy to his relief area.
4 p.m.	Feed Teddy. Let him out within twenty minutes.
6 p.m.	Take Teddy to his relief area.
8 p.m.	Take Teddy to his relief area.
10 p.m.	Take Teddy to his relief area.

Factor in the times Teddy naps and plays. You should take him to his relief area more often when he is more active. Most housetraining accidents occur when there is more commotion in the home, such as when the kids come home from school or on the weekends when more family members are around.

You should go out through the same door every time. This helps with the housetraining process. If you wish him to eliminate in a specific place, be sure to take him there every time. This helps, too, because his scent is there, and this will encourage him to leave more scent in the same spot. Eventually he will go there on his own, but initially you will have to go with him.

Small breed puppies have to relieve themselves more often than larger breed puppies. Many apartment and condominium dwellers tend to have smaller breed dogs, and also tend to want them to learn to relieve themselves indoors on potty pads. This can present a confusing situation for a young dog, because the definition of the proper relief area is not as clear as indoors versus outdoors.

The more clearly the relief area is defined, the faster the pup will learn where to go. If you must set up an indoor relief area, start by making it as large as possible. For example, cover an entire bathroom area with the potty pads, or the whole interior of an exercise pen. As pup learns that this particular room is where he is to relieve himself, he will become more specific about the actual spots within the room where he eliminates and defecates. As he does, you can reduce the amount of padding to those specific locations. However, I would always recommend that he goes outside through the same door, to the same place . . . often.

If Teddy tends to drink a lot of water and then urinate shortly afterward, limit his water intake in the evening *only*. Take the water away around 8 or 9 p.m. Give him an ice cube in his water dish at night. He'll have loads of fun with it. Ice cubes are especially good for teething dogs. *Never* completely take away Teddy's water. He needs to replenish his moisture regularly and should always have access to some form of fresh water.

Besides keeping to a schedule, you'll need to teach Teddy to eliminate on command. This is done with CPR. Consistently use the same verbal cue to request the behavior (the visual cue is going outdoors or to his potty pads). Use repetition to make sure he understands and learns.

1. Take Teddy to his relief area through the same door every time.
2. Once there, say his potty word over and over.
3. When he goes, praise him.
4. When he's done, click and reward. A reward can be food, a toy, or play.
5. As he learns, give him more freedom in your home—under your watchful eye, of course.

If you take Teddy outside and he does not relieve himself after ten minutes, return inside and place him in his crate. This will keep him from relieving himself in an incorrect place. After twenty to thirty minutes, take him to his relief area again and repeat the process. Most likely he'll go. After a day or two of repetition, he will be pottying on command. No more long waits in the rain and cold. Yeah!

Using this method, you will have guided Teddy to learn appropriate house manners without having to punish him. It is all done with redirection and reward. This is far easier than training your dog through punishment, and you maintain a more positive relationship. Slapping your dog after he has eliminated in the wrong place only makes him afraid of you. Dogs rarely identify past actions with present punishment—even if the past was just a few minutes ago. You may see a guilty expression on his face, but this is simply a reaction to your anger. Teddy reads your emotions through your body language, vocal tones, and smell, so even if you are not yelling, Teddy knows you're angry (how could you not be when your pup has just urinated on the carpet?). Most often, his reaction is fear.

Through constant observation and by following a schedule, Teddy will fully understand house training without ever having been punished.

Learning a Signal

Teddy is eager to communicate with you. He doesn't understand why you do not respond to his signals. He sits and stares at you, scratches at your leg, sits at the door, or turns in circles sniffing. Giving up, Teddy goes behind the couch for privacy. Oops! An accident!

Why punish him? He *tried* to tell you. *You* didn't listen. Did you expect him to sit beside you and say (in English), "Hey, Mom, I really need to potty right now. Can you take me outside?" He *did* do that—only he was speaking canine.

There is a clear way of bridging this communication gap: Teach Teddy to ring a bell every time he needs to go outside. Just as he learns through the tone of your voice and the consistent use of verbal and visual cues, he can also learn the meaning of the bell.

You'll need a cowbell or a large jingle bell. Hang it on the doorknob of the door through which you take Teddy out to his relief area.

1. Before you go outside, rub a small bit of cheese on the bell.
2. Tap the bell with the target stick.
3. When Teddy touches it, he'll smell the cheese and want to lick it off.
4. Click as he begins to eat the cheese.
5. Take him outside to his relief area.
6. Say his potty word until he does his business.
7. Click and reward, then play with him for a few minutes or allow him to return to the house with a bit of freedom for a while—within limits, of course.

Tap the bell with the target stick.

When Teddy targets the bell, it will ring.

Teddy will get the idea within a week or less that ringing the bell gets him a potty trip. The sound of the bell has literally bridged the language gap. He rings the bell, the bell makes a bridging sound, and he is rewarded by going to his relief area, where he is further rewarded with another bridging sound and a treat upon eliminating. That's two rewards in one for eliminating in the right place!

This works for dogs of any age or breed. I've taught it to Shih Tzu pups and old Labrador Retrievers, teenage Boxers, and Miniature Poodle babies. Use a bell appropriate to the size of the dog and hang it low enough so the dog can easily nose it and make it ring. As Teddy grows, shorten the length of rope, raising the bell.

This is also a great way of communication while traveling. The door Teddy is used to going out through isn't available, but he will recognize his bell hanging from the hotel room door and will ring it when he needs to relieve himself. To prevent accidents, also take the bell with you when you visit family and friends.

JUMPING UP

Dogs aren't born with a desire to jump up on people. This is a learned behavior. Puppies jump on one another all the time. It is a form of play. It is also a way to make demands. Teddy jumps on you because he is rewarded for doing so. The reward could be your touch, your voice, or the mere fun of it—a game to get your response.

There are as many types of rewards as there are situations in which to give them. Teddy can be rewarded with a treat, toy, touch, your voice, going through a gate, chasing another dog, chasing a cat, chasing a squirrel . . . and the list goes on.

If you really wish to stop this behavior, first analyze how Teddy is being rewarded for doing it. What is your usual reaction when a dog jumps up? You touch him. You speak to him. He's got his front paws on you.

You need to redirect Teddy to a more appropriate behavior that will be equally rewarding. Instead of jumping up to greet you, how about if he sits? This is easily taught with clicker training.

By now Teddy should know the sit command. Incorporate this into his redirection.

1. When Teddy is crouching on his haunches, preparing to jump on you, tell him to sit.

2. As he sits, click, praise, and reward.

3. Crouch to his level and pet him.

Crouch to the dog's level to give him attention.

Insist that your dog sit for attention.

If Teddy has already jumped on you, step back and away. Teddy will fall back to all fours on the floor. When he does so, click and pet him. If he doesn't, give the sit command, click, and pet when he sits. In a short time Teddy will learn that he receives petting if he sits and he receives nothing if he jumps.

This may not always work if your dog has a tendency to jump on other people, because they will not implement these training procedures. Instead, they will touch the dog, speak to him . . . reward him. In this situation, Teddy has learned that he may not jump on you but he may jump on others. To remedy this, you will need a training device or aid. You can use a head halter to prevent Teddy from jumping and to teach him to sit instead. You'll need to practice this as people arrive; perhaps you can enlist a friend to help with training sessions.

1. Take Teddy to the door, wearing his head halter.

2. Place him in a sit-stay near the door, but in a position where he is not blocking the door.

Have your dog perform a sit-stay at the door.

3. Put your foot on the leash. Not so tight as to cause pressure while Teddy sits, but enough so that he can't pop up.

4. As the person walks in the door, praise Teddy while he sits. Make sure the person does not greet Teddy but just walks past him and in.

5. When the person has passed Teddy, click and reward.

Another training device you can use for this problem is what I call the no-jump box. It is a metal box or can with pennies inside that makes a loud rattling noise when shaken. I use a small, round paint can with fifteen pennies inside.

Lay the middle of the leash on the floor and put your foot on it.

When the dog jumps up, shake the can up and down only once or twice as you use a low, growly "no." When you shake it, the noise will *startle* your dog. While some dogs will run and hide, others will simply replace all four feet on the ground.

Any can will work as a no-jump box, as long as you can close it securely with the pennies inside.

There is a very small percentage of dogs for which the device doesn't work at all, but you won't know until you try.

When the dog has all four feet on the ground, request a sit. When he complies, reward him with praise and a click, followed by attention in the form of touch or a treat. Teddy will quickly learn that he hears a horrible sound when he jumps up but receives the attention he craves when he sits. With clear communication of this sort, Teddy learns to stop jumping on everyone. It's about the quickest fix there is for a habitual jumper. If it is used too much, however, your dog will become indifferent to the sound, and may even think it's a toy.

Achieving the goal of Teddy sitting calmly as the person comes in and walks past him may take several training sessions. Some dogs are so happy to see people that they can barely control themselves. Break the behavior down into manageable parts so that you can set your dog up for success instead of constant correction.

Teaching your dog to sit at the door will help with many behavioral issues, such as charging the door when the doorbell rings, charging the door to welcome visitors, and charging the door to get outside. Performing a sit-stay at the door will teach him to control his behavior in all situations. He will learn how positive it can be to remain seated as he is praised and rewarded.

If the situation becomes uncontrollable, take Teddy into a different room and work on some exercises at which he excels. Always end training sessions on a positive note, never working beyond your dog's threshold. This means frequent breaks when you and Teddy can relax and regain your composure. Otherwise you'll be building up a situation in which every time the doorbell rings, Teddy becomes anxious.

BARKING

No dog is 100 percent quiet. Dogs bark to express themselves in many ways. It's a form of language, just as we use our voices to speak. Barking may not have as many nuances as human speech, but different barks have distinct tones with specific meanings. You cannot expect your dog never to bark, and that should not be your training goal. In fact, it's a good thing for him to bark to alert you to visitors or intruders.

The key to enjoying your dog's vocalizations is to keep them under control. It is very annoying to have a dog who barks out the window at every moving thing or every subtle noise—or worse, at nothing at all. It's also intimidating to have a dog who barks at other dogs while walking down the street. This can incite passing dogs into aggressive displays. Most annoying is a dog who is barking while you are on the phone or visiting with someone. This is a dog who has learned to bark for attention.

Yelling at your dog to stop barking does not work. In his mind, you are merely joining in the bark fest, plus giving Teddy attention, which increases the likelihood that he will continue to bark. You most certainly cannot call your dog to come to you and then correct him for barking. He'll never want to come to you again. Hitting your dog is out of the question, as is throwing something at him. The more negative your response to excessive barking, the worse the problem and the more you increase the rift between you and your dog.

There are several specific reasons why a dog will bark excessively. He might be protecting his territory, seeking attention, fearful, or playing. Each situation should be corrected and controlled differently. In general, as with all inappropriate behavior, you need to redirect Teddy to good behavior by clicking and rewarding the moment he does as you wish.

Territorial/Protective Barking

This is the most common reason for excessive barking. Teddy sees or hears an intruder and alerts the rest of the pack—you. Unfortunately, Teddy continues to bark even when the intruder is gone, or if you have allowed the "intruder" (an accepted visitor, in this case) into your home. Teddy also barks at the dog being walked across the street, or at the dog who plays in a nearby yard. Walking with Teddy is so difficult that you choose not to do it at all, which not only decreases his much-needed exercise but also breaks down the bond the two of you have cherished. Being unable to give your dog appropriate exercise leads to more problems than I can describe in this book.

Regardless of what Teddy is barking at, you need to control his outbursts and redirect him to the appropriate use of his voice. He should let you know when someone nears your home or enters it without your consent. He naturally wants to protect you from people with bad intentions. However, who the bad people are is *your* choice to make, not his.

When Teddy is barking at the door, give him a word that means he's done enough barking. I usually say "quiet" or "enough." Then redirect Teddy by making a novel sound, such as ringing a bell or squeaking a toy. Throwing a toy is also helpful. When your dog stops barking, click and reward him. He is on his way to learning how to turn it off. As he understands your cue, ask him to keep quiet for longer and longer periods of time before the click and reward. Soon Teddy will respond quickly to the cue to stop barking because he will be looking forward to getting good things.

It is not always this easy, though. Many dogs simply do not respect their people enough to respond. They believe they are in charge and must take action against the intruder. You will need to use a head halter with such a dog. You should also be working on obedience training. Teddy's respect for you goes hand in hand with his listening to your commands regardless of distractions. You cannot get control of his barking without overall control of his behavior.

Barking is often a self-rewarding behavior, as well, making it difficult to redirect your dog. In this situation you'll need to use a training tool. The best tool for handling territorial barking is a head halter. You can physically redirect Teddy, then click and reward the moment you made him perform correctly.

Curing this type of barking problem cannot always be done with purely positive reinforcement. A head halter will give you the leverage you need to reinforce your commands.

1. When Teddy barks, tell him to sit.
2. If he responds, he will most likely stop barking. Click and reward, then go on to a stay or another exercise.

3. If he doesn't respond, look in his eyes as you pull forward and up on the leash. Say "no" as you continually look in his eyes until he looks away. The upward pull will place Teddy in a sit.

4. The moment your dog's behind is on the floor, praise, click and reward. Then go on to another exercise, until his anxiety over whatever caused the barking is no longer apparent.

Pull forward and upward on the leash as you look into his eyes.

Attention-Seeking Barking

The dog barks and his human companions jump. From those dogs who speak out at being placed in a crate to those who take over telephone conversations or visits with friends, these are all dogs who have learned that barking will give them their owner's complete attention. For the attention seeker, even yelling at them is enough to reinforce the behavior.

Redirecting them to a positive behavior is key to curing this problem. The behavior can be sitting or lying down, performing a stay, rolling over, or turning in circles. It doesn't matter. The alternate behavior (whatever it is) must be rewarded if that is what you wish Teddy to do when he needs you. Then again, you do have a life and you can't always drop everything when your dog desires. Ultimately, this alternate behavior must be under your control. I have found that the best way to teach Teddy patience is to have him perform a down-stay. This keeps him busy—but quiet—when you are busy.

If at all possible, you need to ignore Teddy when he barks for attention. If he's lonely in his crate at bedtime, put cotton in your ears. If he's angling for you to pick him up, ignore him. However, if by chance he does something else (something quiet), such as lying down, you must immediately click and reward him with attention. Teddy will quickly figure out what he did that earned him the attention he craved. Be consistent with this and soon your dog will be lying down when you are speaking on the phone or socializing. Always be sure to reward him for this behavior, or he'll go back to barking for the reward.

Play Barking

This is not a situation you can totally control. On the one hand, you do not want to stifle Teddy's playful tendencies. It's fun to watch him run and play. That's part of having a dog. However, some dogs are annoyingly loud during play. If you want a quiet dog, do some breed research and choose wisely.

Otherwise, you will need to either put up with the play barking or fill Teddy's mouth with a chew toy. There are many fun chew toys on the market. Many of them are interactive, which means Teddy must turn or pull at the toy to get a treat. This will keep your dog busy for long periods of time and, best of all, quiet.

Fill your dog's mouth with a toy to stop his play barking.

CHEWING AND MOUTHING

Dogs chew for many reasons. The main one is just to pass the time. Dogs do not read books, rarely watch television, and often spend long hours alone waiting for their families to return home from work or school. What's a dog to do? Chew.

Some dogs chew excessively. This is due either to boredom or anxiety. It's similar to people who eat excessively, which is also usually due to boredom or anxiety. Different species but similar behavior.

If you got Teddy as a pup and have worked consistently with him, it will be easy to redirect inappropriate chewing behavior. You'll simply take away the wrong thing and replace it with the right toy, praising as he chews on it. This is easy reinforcement.

If you got your dog from a shelter or rescue group, he likely hasn't had the benefit of early training. In fact, many of the dogs in shelters end up there because of chewing issues. In this case, the problem cannot just be redirected. It must be confronted.

Supervision is key. When you cannot be with Teddy, he must be contained in an area where he cannot chew anything inappropriate. Within this area he

Replace the wrong object with a dog toy.

Unless you were planning to redecorate your home, you cannot write off inappropriate chewing behavior as something your dog will outgrow. You are risking not only your belongings—even those new carpets and windowsills you plan to put in after your dog is an adult—but also your own dog's health, because if he chews and swallows something toxic, bulky, or sharp, it can be fatal.

Bad habits need to be dealt with head-on. If this means confinement every time you leave home, so be it. This will be safer for your dog in many ways. First of all, it gives him a safe place to rest when the pack (your family) is scattered, making him feel more secure. And this will reduce the incidence of separation anxiety. Second, it keeps your household goods intact, which helps you maintain a positive relationship with your dog.

should have plenty of chew toys, including interactive ones, to promote his desire to play with them. The more rewarding the toy, the more likely it is to grab and retain Teddy's attention.

When you can directly observe Teddy, keep him with you at all times. Make sure there are at least three toys he really values within his reach. As he plays with them, praise him. Play with him using those toys; dogs love to have play partners. Just the fact that you are playing with him will be highly rewarding.

If Teddy starts toward an inappropriate chewing object, such as a lamp cord or the television remote control, first say "no," then redirect him to his toy by moving it around. Dogs would rather go after moving objects than stationary ones.

Your dog must have access to several fun chew toys.

The fact that you are playing with him will immediately reinforce the value of that object. If you are holding your clicker, go ahead and click as he redirects his attention to the correct chew toy. The toy itself will be his reward.

You deal with mouthing of your hands in a similar way. Mouthing can either be an attention-seeking behavior or a test of dominance. Regardless of the reason, redirect Teddy to an appropriate object and reward him with praise, touch, and play. Always convey to your dog that he can obtain your attention faster through appropriate actions than through inappropriate ones.

Play with your dog using the toy you want him to chew.

DIGGING

Digging is one of a dog's favorite pastimes. It's the activity that keeps on giving. From making a bed to burying bones to covering oneself in dirt, there is hardly a canine game that doesn't involve digging. You cannot take the dig out of the dog; however, you can direct him to an appropriate area.

A backyard sandbox can be just as much fun for Teddy as it is for your children. A pile of dirt or mulch can be equally appealing. Just be sure Teddy has someplace acceptable to dig and that you reward him whenever he uses it. The reward can be praise, but an even higher value reward is to join in the game.

There are several ways of resolving a digging problem without having to be constantly watching Teddy. The success of each depends mostly on your dog. While

I have sectioned my yard into a dog play area and a garden area. This has translated into an area where the dogs can dig and an area where they cannot. Initially, I had to enclose them in their area to prevent them from destroying the garden. Once they learned where they may play and where they may not, I have been able to keep the garden gate open. This may not always be the case, though; with many dogs, you'll always have to keep the garden gate closed. However, sectioning off an area for your dog will help maintain your sanity and give your dog a place where he can be free to express himself.

some dogs might be very sensitive to sounds or smells, others don't care. For dogs who aren't deterred by the following suggestions, you will simply need to monitor their outdoor activities and guide them in the right direction.

Some ideas to prevent digging:

1. Control the moles in your yard. Many dogs will dig when they smell these critters and see their tunnel pathways—which have already churned up the dirt, making it more appealing to dig in.

2. Make sure your dog has a happy home life with plenty of socialization with other dogs. Dogs will dig out of their yards to go socialize.

3. Put a kiddie wading pool in your yard, filled with water. This will reduce the need to dig on hot days to find a cool place to lie down.

4. Put a hard surface in the dog area, such as stone dust. Dogs prefer to dig in softer surfaces. If you do this, also provide an area that does offer a digging surface so Teddy can exercise in his preferred manner.

Once the digging has begun, you can try the following:

1. Pour vinegar into already existing holes. Many dogs hate the smell and will avoid those areas. Because most dogs prefer to dig in specific spots, this can prove successful in reducing the digging problem.

2. Put a balloon in the hole and cover it with loose dirt. When the dog digs again in that spot, he'll hear a scary pop that might put him off the behavior. Dogs don't like holes that bark at them.

3. Use your no-jump box, giving it a shake when he digs. Click and reward when he stops and turns his attention to a toy.

Dig on Command

You can also transform your dog's digging into an on-demand behavior, using either capturing or shaping. The capture might prove easiest, since you simply click and reward when Teddy is digging in the appropriate spot. He might stop for a bit after that, wondering what he did to earn him the reward, but if you return his attention to the digging, you can reinforce the behavior by clicking again. After two to three repetitions, Teddy will know why he is being rewarded and will strive to earn more.

At this point you'll need to add a verbal and/or visual cue, or else Teddy will be creating a lunar landscape whenever he wants to earn rewards. Once he identifies the cue with his digging behavior, he will eventually stop digging until you give him the cue.

Shaping a dig will take some time, since you need to break it down into very small parts. These parts might be:

1. Teach Teddy to go to the digging spot.
2. Teach Teddy to sniff the ground where you wish him to dig.
3. Teach Teddy to move his foreleg while sniffing.
4. Teach Teddy to use his foreleg to move some dirt.
5. Gradually increase the amount of dirt Teddy must move to get his click and treat.

Each of these parts needs to be further broken down to achieve the behavior. Sometimes it is easier to teach a complex behavior by teaching the last part first. This is called back-chaining. For example, suppose you wish to teach Teddy to run across the room, give Grandma a kiss, and then return to you with a ball. You might begin by teaching Teddy to give you a ball. Next you teach him how to pick up the ball and bring it to you. After this you teach him to give Grandma a kiss, then to pick up the ball and bring it to you. Finally, you teach Teddy to run across a room to give Grandma the kiss, followed by the remainder of the exercise. This is a back-chain.

The approach you use to teaching your dog to dig will depend on your dog. If he is a natural digger, you won't have to do much more than create an environment where he will dig and capture the behavior. If Teddy is not a natural digger, you can try to create the environment by burying a treat or toy in a very shallow hole or under a throw rug. Teddy is certain to want the treat, so he will figure out that he must dig it up. As he digs, you capture the moment with a click and a reward.

If Teddy does not care about digging up anything, you'll never have to worry about holes in your yard, so you may not want to teach your dog to become so creative.

Bury a toy under a throw rug.

Capture the moment the dog digs for the toy.

Dogs love to be surrounded by your scent.

STEALING

Before you can solve this problem, you need to understand why it occurs. Is Teddy taking food from tables or counters? Is he taking dirty laundry from the hamper? Does he take a household item and run with it? The best way to deal with this behavior depends on what the reward is for Teddy.

Stealing food is obvious: The mere act of obtaining the food is the reward. The dirty laundry and household items are a little bit less obvious. Teddy's goal with the dirty laundry may be to keep your smell nearby, or to lure you into a game of tag. Stealing the household item can be self-rewarding if he uses it as a chew object. Or, as in the case of the laundry, he may be trying to instigate a game.

To resolve these behaviors you must make them aversive instead of rewarding. You can also redirect Teddy to more appropriate behavior for which he will receive a reward.

There are other considerations as well. Does Teddy do these things in front of you or behind your back? You can bet that after an initial verbal reprimand, Teddy will rarely do it in front of you. He knows better. To prevent it from happening behind your back, you will need to keep your dog with you at all times, on a leash if need be. This will prevent the behavior while teaching Teddy that he is far happier remaining at your side, shadowing your movements. There is no need to steal your scent-filled clothing from the laundry basket when he can have you near him. There is no need to steal a household object when there are many dog toys to chose from near him. And, if he lies quietly or plays nicely with his toys, he will receive rewards in the form of praise and caresses.

Regardless of how consistent you are at keeping an eye on your dog, Teddy will still steal things when he simply cannot resist the temptation. That juicy holiday turkey on the table while everyone is in the family room is just too tempting! Nobody will really miss those bread crumbs—or the entire loaf—on the counter, will they?

You will need to set up a way to teach Teddy that giving in to temptation is not fun. A scat mat, which is an electrified plastic mat, is just the thing. When Teddy jumps on it, he will receive an electrical tingle on his paws. He will be surprised (not hurt), and

A scat mat will help convince your dog that tempting morsels are not as desirable as they seem.

this should be enough to convince him that counter-surfing is not rewarding. If you can catch him in the act of getting down, when he puts all four on the floor, call him to you and reward him for coming.

Most behavioral issues can be redirected using clicker training and clear communication. Addressing them takes a bit of your time, but far less time than you will spend scolding Teddy over the course of his life. And the results are well worth it. You will have a dog who can be reliable at home alone or out in public—one you adore being with and who adores being with you.

Chapter 6

Off and Running

While it is great to have a dog who obeys your commands at home off leash and outdoors on a leash, it is far better for Teddy to also be reliable off leash in public places. You never know when you'll need him to be obedient under these circumstances. It could be after off-leash play at a dog park, while hiking in the mountains, or when someone accidentally leaves your door or gate open. Teddy must know how to comply with your requests, without a leash, in all situations.

You began training indoors in a quiet room without a leash. You added the leash when you moved outdoors, with its inherent distractions. The leash was the only way to enable you to follow through when Teddy did not respond as he should. Now it's time to graduate to not needing a leash at any time, anywhere.

Of course, there are leash laws in urban and suburban areas that you must follow, but even in these situations you may want to take Teddy off the leash while you're in your own backyard and when you're involved in outdoor activities. Even urban areas like New York City have off-leash dog parks. It's tough to play fetch or play with other dogs on a leash. It's also no fun to always be on a leash when you're out camping or hiking. (Although it's mandatory to leash your dog in state parks, it's not mandatory in wildlife management areas.)

There are four phases to training Teddy to work without a leash around distractions and at distances greater than the length of any leash. Throughout the process, I combine on-leash control with the click and treat marker to ensure that Teddy continues to enjoy his training sessions.

Everything is still accomplished by breaking down the final goal into smaller goals, to build reliability and clear understanding, as follows:

Phase 1. Increase the distance between you and Teddy to twenty feet, on-leash.

Phase 2.   Drop the twenty-foot leash and increase the distance even more.

Phase 3.   Use a six-foot leash merely for backup, if required. Use a twenty-foot leash if you're in a large area with many distractions.

Phase 4.   Teddy is off leash with a very short leash attached to his collar—called a pull tab—as both a reminder and a back-up.

INCREASE THE DISTANCE

Increasing distance only pertains to the stay exercises and come. (There would be no reason to increase your dog's distance from you on the heel, since the whole point is to have him walking alongside you.) So in Phase 1 you'll increase the distance on the sit-stay, down-stay and stand-stays, and have him come when called from up to twenty feet away.

Make sure you always gradually increase your distance and that you never go straight out or backward, because this essentially gives the cue for come. Instead, walk around your dog as you move away. If your dog sees you moving backward, as you did when you were first teaching him to come, he will leave his stay position to come and sit in front of you. By walking around him as you increase the distance, you are not giving him any visual cues to come and you can increase your distance without being obvious about it.

Here's how we will shape this behavior.

1. Put Teddy in a sit-stay, then increase the distance as you step away from six to ten feet. Vary the exercise by sometimes returning to Teddy's side after a stay, then click and reward. Other times, have Teddy come, then click and reward. Or click and reward after a finish. The more you vary the exercise, the more attentive Teddy will remain.

2. From the down-stay, increase the distance you step away from six to ten feet. Vary the exercises as outlined in step 1.

3. From the stand-stay, increase the distance you step away from six to ten feet. I recommend you do not call your dog to come from a stand-stay, because it is very easy to move while standing and a dog who is prone to anticipating your commands *will* move. Make sure Teddy is very solid on this exercise before you ask him to come. You can continue to increase your distance, though.

If Teddy begins anticipating or moving out of his stays, return to the distance at which he was responding appropriately and work at that level for a while. Once your dog is steady on stays and come from ten feet, move out to fourteen or fifteen feet. Then go on to the end of the twenty-foot leash.

Gradually increase the distance as you walk around your dog.

Once you can move away ten feet, try adding another four to five feet of distance.

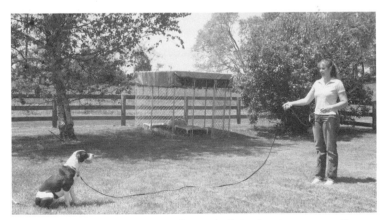

Finally, you can stretch out to the end of the leash as you walk around Teddy.

When you're gathering up the long leash, bring your arms out and slide the leash through your hands.

Take hold of the leash and bring your arms together.

Continue until the leash is completely gathered.

Hold the extra leash in the hand opposite the side on which you walk your dog.

If Teddy leaves his stay either because he was distracted or because he's anticipating the come exercise, always use your verbal correction "no" and take hold of the leash near his collar to lead him back to the spot where you first told him to stay. Then go back to the distance at which Teddy was staying reliably. If he still leaves the stay position, move even closer to him. There may be a distraction he cannot ignore, and you must work again on having him pay attention to you in the presence of that distraction before you can increase your distance.

Teddy comes from twenty feet away.

Build on your successes and do not constantly correct Teddy. One correction means he does not understand the entire exercise. Back up, let him be successful, then move on.

Once you have attained the goal of being able to move entirely around Teddy at a distance of twenty feet and he will come when called regardless of where you are stationed around him, move on to the next step.

DROP THE LEASH

This may seem like a big step, especially when you're outdoors and not in a fenced-in area, but to Teddy it is meaningless. He most likely will not realize that you are not holding the other end of the leash. We won't make a big deal out of dropping the leash. In fact, we will be doing it surreptitiously.

1. Put Teddy in a stay (it doesn't matter whether it's a sit-stay or a down-stay).
2. Work your way out to the end of the leash as you walk around Teddy.
3. When you are behind him, drop the leash and keep walking. Do not lay it down, because Teddy will see this visual movement and be tempted to come to you—and you don't want to give him mixed signals. Keep everything clear, concise, and positive.
4. Make a complete circle around Teddy and return to the spot where you dropped the end of the leash.
5. Step on the end of the leash.
6. Call Teddy to come and sit in front of you.
7. When he arrives, click and reward. Or do a finish, then click and reward.

Practice this from both the sit-stay and the down-stay. Every other exercise, return to the heel position, click and reward, then go on to the heel or another command. You can even do another stay.

Drop the leash as you move behind your dog.

Step on the end of the leash before calling your dog to come.

If you want Teddy to heel, you will need to gather the leash quickly and efficiently. This can be a problem, though, when you're working with a twenty-foot leash. You can take hold of the leash near Teddy's collar, go into the heel exercise, and gather the leash as you walk. Always gather from the end closest to your dog and out to the other end, looping it, then stretching out your arm for another grab (as described earlier in this chapter).

Or you can take the leash near your dog's collar and do a finish. You can then go on into the heeling exercise and gather the leash as I've just described, or simply let it drag behind you. When you stop you can gather it. Allowing the leash to drag behind you won't do anything besides get it dirty.

Which exercise you use depends on your ability to perform more than one task at a time. Multitasking isn't for everyone, and during the learning process you might not wish to add on any extras. Keeping things simple for both yourself and your dog will free your mind to learn. Whatever works best for you is the path you should take.

Take the leash near your dog's collar.

You should also give yourselves frequent break times. Teddy needs to relax his mind and body so he can maintain a positive attitude. It does not hurt to stop working and engage in a short grooming session or just relax in the shade. Frequent breaks offer you time to think about what you have just done and how you can continue making progress, as well. As with gathering a long leash, it can be difficult to think of the next step or goal while you are engaged in a physical activity.

When you're practicing with a dropped leash, be sure to do the come from various directions. You do not want Teddy to believe he is only called to you when you are standing in front of him. Practice from both sides and from behind him.

If you have trees, bushes or other objects in your training area, try hiding behind these during the stays. Peek out and check on your dog. If he is still where you told him to stay, click and return to him, giving him his reward. On other occasions, have him come to you at your hiding place. This is the start of teaching Teddy to stay and come when you are out of sight.

As with all exercises, break this one down into smaller goals. Begin by being only partially hidden. As Teddy accepts the fact that he must respond to the commands even when part of you is out of sight, you can gradually increase how much of you is hidden. Through this process, Teddy learns that he must continue to respond to your cues even if he can't see you. When the exercise is complete, click and reward; the bridge and result must always remain consistent if you want your dog to continue to offer appropriate responses to the initial cues, whether or not you are present.

Hide behind trees and peek around to see how your dog is doing.

GREATER DISTANCE, DROPPED LEASH

This third phase is very similar to the previous one, except the leash is always dragging on the ground without a clear connection between Teddy's collar and your hand. You can use either the twenty-foot leash or a lightweight six-foot leash. The length depends on Teddy's reliability at this point. If your dog has a tendency to bolt after squirrels or other dogs, you might want to keep the twenty-foot leash (there's more to grab when your dog takes off). If this is rarely the case, the lightweight six-foot leash might be fine. Make sure Teddy is wearing a leash appropriate to his temperament. In general, it is a good idea to keep a longer leash on a faster moving dog, such as a herding breed or a sighthound. (Yes, sighthounds can learn to work off leash.) Do what is best for you and your dog at the time.

Regardless of the length of the leash, you must not show that you are holding it. Dogs know these things. They understand the connection between your ability to control them and you having the leash in your hand. At this point in training it should not make any difference, because Teddy should work equally well for you indoors or out and in the presence of myriad distractions. I merely consider myself a *safety person*. The last thing I want to hear about are dogs running loose on a busy street. It can happen to anyone, even the best-trained dogs. So be safe.

Hold the leash in the hand opposite the side where your dog walks, with the slack behind your back.

To make your dog believe there is no connection between you and him, put the leash behind your back and hold it in the hand opposite the side at which Teddy heels. So if Teddy heels on your left, hold the very end of the leash in your right hand with the rest of it trailing behind your back.

If Teddy is at all bothered by the weight of a trailing twenty-foot leash, you can either gather a little more of it or use a shorter leash. There may also be times when he steps on the leash. This can bother some dogs, especially if they are still working with a head halter or other training device. You should not try to achieve this level of off-leash work until you have first weaned your dog off the training device. At this point in training, Teddy should only have to wear his regular neck collar or body harness.

Phase 3 Heeling

1. Begin with Teddy in the heel position.

2. Hold the leash behind your back in the hand opposite the side at which Teddy heels. Hold only the very end or the leash handle. Allow the remainder of the leash to rest on the ground.

3. Go forward into the heel.

4. Stop often, click and reward. Turns are also helpful in keeping Teddy's attention on you. If Teddy lags behind, slap your leg and use enthusiastic words of encouragement. Do not give the heel command again.

Stay

1. Stop walking and have Teddy sit or lie down.

2. Tell him to stay and drop the leash at his feet. If you feel the need to maintain some safety, enlist the help of a friend to stand on the leash as you move away. Or you can have Teddy perform the stay near a fence or a tree and tie the end of the leash around a post or a branch.

3. Gradually increase the distance and time of each stay, and start briefly hiding behind objects in the area.

4. Either return to your dog, click and reward, or call him to come, then click and reward. If you tied him to something, be sure you call him to come from a distance the leash will reach.

Drop the leash at your dog's feet while he is in the down-stay.

Drop the leash at your dog's feet while he is in the sit-stay.

Hide while dog remains in a stay with the leash at his feet.

Come

Do the come at this stage the same way you did it in Phase 2, except you will not be standing on the leash. When Teddy comes to you, the leash will be dragging behind him, so make sure this doesn't bother him. The last thing you want is to give your dog a bad experience as he comes to you.

As with all exercises, gradually shape the final behavior by starting small. Begin the dropped leash recall from just ten or fifteen feet away. When Teddy is reliable at this distance from all angles, increase the distance to twenty feet. You can move farther away as Teddy becomes more reliable.

Also practice out-of-sight exercises by calling your dog to come to you when he cannot see you. If he does not respond immediately, show yourself to him and encourage him to complete the exercise. As he comes to you, praise him enthusiastically. Click and reward when he sits in front of you.

Teddy comes from a distance.

Your dog must ignore distractions in the area and come to you when he is called.

Distraction Proofing

Even at this advanced stage of training there will be things and events that distract Teddy. He is not a robot. No dog is perfect all the time. However, Teddy should be very responsive to a verbal correction at this point. The verbal correction alone should be enough to return his attention to you. If not, he is not yet ready to have you drop the leash.

From a distance you can guide Teddy with your verbal cues. As he is performing well, tell him "good boy" in a happy, enthusiastic tone of voice. When he becomes distracted, use your verbal correction tone. The moment he is back on track, praise enthusiastically again.

WE'RE OFF!

We made it. Teddy responds reliably to your verbal and visual cues. Now all leashes can come off. One thing, though: You might want to attach a little pull tab to his collar. This reminds him that he is still under your control in some way, and also gives you the extra insurance of having something to take hold of if the need arises. The last thing anyone should do is to grab a dog by his collar. This is very threatening and will not achieve the control you are seeking. Instead, it will elicit a fearful response.

The pull tab should be four to six inches long; shorter if you have a toy breed. The tab should be long enough to take hold of but not so long that it drags on the ground or flops against Teddy's legs.

Go through all the same obedience exercises, only back up a bit on your criteria. When heeling, shorten the length of time between stops. Do many turns and changes of pace. This keeps Teddy on his toes and having fun. When you are

A pull tab attached to the regular collar will serve as a reminder to your dog.

working on stay and come, shorten the time and distance. As Teddy performs well, increase these criteria again. The same goes for exposure to distractions. Begin without anything too tempting nearby and gradually increase the distraction level as Teddy becomes reliable.

It's also a good idea to shorten the actual training sessions and offer several relaxing breaks. The better Teddy performs, the more free time he should receive. He's earned it. During these breaks you can add a few learning games, such as having him come to you, then allowing him to go play again. Or you can play a controlled game of fetch in which Teddy must remain at your side as you throw the toy and not retrieve it until you release him. One game for dogs who love to dig is to bury a toy and then allow Teddy to go dig it up. This gives your dog a chance to use his strong desire to dig in a managed setting, where he will be rewarded for doing so—but only when you say it's OK.

OUTDOOR ACTIVITIES OFF LEASH

I mentioned a few possible activities already: fetching, digging, and calling your dog to come from long distances and out of sight. The many things you can do with a well-trained dog are too numerous to list in this book, but I'll mentioned a few that I enjoy doing with my dogs. If my dogs were not trained to listen without a leash or any actual *hands-on* guidance, the activity would not be as enjoyable—and in many cases, not even possible. That's because they often must behave in public areas that have a lot of pedestrian or vehicle traffic.

In addition to the ones mentioned here, there are so many more activities you and Teddy can enjoy outdoors and in public places. With imagination there can be no limits. A well-trained dog is a pleasure to have with you and a joy for all to behold.

Play in the Park

Whether you live in an urban, suburban, or rural area, Teddy will love a romp in the park. This can be a great social event for both of you. Not only will Teddy meet and play with other dogs, but you can talk with other dog lovers while

Working near a busy park is a good way to teach your dog to pay attention.

watching him play. Movies have been made about this. Single? What better way to meet someone with similar interests? Married? What better way to spend some quality time with your spouse?

The more Teddy is able to play, the fewer behavior problems you will see. A well-exercised dog is less likely to have chewing issues due to boredom and pent-up energy. A well-socialized dog will be less likely to show aggression to other dogs. You can also use this environment as a place to work with Teddy on distraction proofing. Parks are filled with dogs, people, children, squirrels, and other wildlife.

The best place to begin with teaching Teddy to pay attention in the park is to do the distraction-proofing exercises in the following order:

1. Begin working with Teddy from the moment he steps out of the car in the parking lot. If you walked to the park from home, training begins the moment the leash is put on for the walk.

2. As Teddy becomes proficient at listening to you, you can gradually move closer to the distraction-filled area. As you get closer to the distraction zone, be sure to click and reward your dog more often. You want to give Teddy the impression that the more distractions there are, the more pleasant the experience when he obeys. Keep in mind that the more difficult the distractions become, the less you should request of your dog. Build upon his successes instead of having to constantly correct him for his failures.

3. When Teddy can perform all his exercises properly on leash, begin working on the long-leash distance exercises. One of the best exercises to practice in the park is the come. Allow him to go play with other dogs, but maintain your hold on the end of the long leash. Call him to you. As he responds, praise him enthusiastically. Click and reward when he arrives. He doesn't

have to sit in front of you every time. Nor does this mean the end of his playtime. Once he arrives and is bridged for doing so, allow him to return to his games. There might be times, however, when continuing the game is more rewarding to him than coming when called. This can present a problem. It is best worked on at this level of training, when you are still holding the leash and can bring Teddy to you when he does not respond to your come command.

4. As your dog performs well at a distance with a dropped leash, move on to his wearing only the pull tab as he works.

If this entire scenario is more than your dog can handle, back up a bit. Go somewhere that does not offer as much distraction. Try to find a place that has only one distraction factor, such as just being away from home; an unfamiliar location can be a huge distraction. Make sure Teddy can handle this before you take him to the park.

Working off leash in the park is an excellent goal. Just make sure off-leash dogs are allowed in your local parks.

If the presence of other dogs is an issue, try to work with your dog in a quieter area where there might be only one dog. Or go around the block, out of sight of the other dogs but still within hearing range. Because a dog's sense of hearing is far better than ours, you can be sure he still hears the other dogs even when you cannot. As Teddy learns that the best rewards come from you, increase the distractions.

Always remember that there may be rewards far greater than food, toys, or your praise and touch. Playing with other dogs and chasing squirrels may be very high on Teddy's reward list. Use these activities as rewards for his good performance. You may not want to do this after just one or two commands, however, or you'll spend the entire training session calling him to come from his playtime. Try having Teddy do a chain of behaviors, such as heel, sit, down-stay, and stand-stay. When he has performed well for a period of time, allow his play reward.

Camping

Camping in the woods or near some water can be a lot of fun with your dog. Teddy will love wading in a creek or fetching a stick from the lake. But he must be off-leash trained if you want to give him the liberty to enjoy the experience. Not only must he remain nearby without your having to keep a constant watch on him, but he must also stay out of the food bags and have some control about entering the tent with muddy feet.

A new behavior that will help you establish temporary boundaries wherever you go is stay here. This means he should remain in the vicinity but not necessarily in one position or in one spot. You'll need to shape stay here into Teddy's behavioral repertoire.

1. Whenever Teddy turns his attention to you, even when he's wandering around, click and reward. At this point he might remain very close and start throwing behaviors at you to see what will earn him a reward. Ignore him. Get him involved in a game of fetch or dipping his toes in the water.

2. When you see Teddy meander off a distance, say his name. When he looks at you, click and reward. Again, he'll come close and try out various behaviors. Again, ignore him or redirect him to a game.

Teddy should look back to check in with you.

3. Repeat step 2 until you see the next behavior in step 4.

4. When Teddy is meandering about and you call his name, he looks at you. Praise him enthusiastically, click, and reward. Repeat this often, because Teddy needs to know he gets better rewards for remaining with you than for following a scent or checking out the next campsite.

5. Now add the command, stay here. Repeat step 4, using the stay here command, as often as necessary until Teddy settles down.

The next new command is stay out. This teaches Teddy to keep out of the tent or any specific area until you tell him he can go in. Stay out is very important for

Camping is far more fun with dogs. The dog must be quick to obey your cues, however. He must also learn new boundaries because you do not want Teddy to wander into other campsites or become lost as he hunts down the source of a scent.

This is especially a liability for hounds, and many hound breeds have been injured or lost due to their lack of training when their owners were using them as hunting companions. More Beagles are lost in this scenario than any other hound breed. Because Beagles have a strong scenting ability and will follow a scent for days, they often leave the area in which they were supposed to be working.

If Teddy is a scenthound, you may want to always keep a long leash on him to keep him from getting lost. This is also a good idea if you have a sighthound. The moment a sighthound sees quick-moving prey, such as deer racing through the forest, he will be off and running before you even notice he's gone.

both your sanity and Teddy's well-being. There are many dangers out in the wilds, from the campfire to snakes to wildlife dens. Your dog must respond quickly and willingly to this command or he is in danger of being injured.

1. As Teddy starts going toward a place or thing you do not wish him to investigate, call out his name. When he looks at you, praise him, click, and reward.

2. Keep an eye on Teddy, and each time he heads toward something dangerous, call his name. When he looks at you, praise him, click, and reward.

3. When Teddy begins looking at you before he heads toward a dangerous place or thing, praise him, click, and reward.

4. Now add the stay out command. When Teddy turns to look at you and leaves the *vicinity* of the bad thing, praise him, click, and reward.

A variation of this cue is leave it, which teaches your dog not to investigate something that might be enticing. The leave it cue is helpful for dogs who love to sniff carcasses or roll in dead fish. Teach it the same way you would teach stay out.

Hiking and Backpacking

Dogs love to romp through the woods and fields. Go on day hikes or overnight trips to give Teddy this opportunity. You'll have as much fun as your dog.

You can use the same cues for hiking as you do for camping. The only difference with the stay here command is that you will be moving and Teddy must learn to remain within a specific distance from you.

1. When Teddy begins to move too far away, call his name. When he looks at you, praise him, click, and reward him when he returns for his treat. If he does not return for his reward, call him using his normal recall cues.

2. Keep an eye on your dog. Any time he begins to move beyond the safe zone, call his name. Always bridge with a click the moment he looks at you, then reward him when he returns to you. If Teddy is more interested in whatever he is hunting than in coming back to you, you must keep him on a leash at all times. The long leash should be fine, as long as you make sure he does not become entangled around trees and brush. Practice the recall exercises every five minutes or so to condition your dog to always be aware of your location and that he cannot wander farther than the leash allows.

3. As Teddy begins to check back with you as he walks, praise, click, and reward every time.

4. Now add the cue stay here. Praise Teddy the entire time he remains close by. Click and reward every couple of minutes, gradually increasing the time span between his bridging sound and the reward.

Your dog should always check in with you as you walk on the trail.

Running with the Horses

Running in the woods alongside horses is a rare opportunity for a dog. Dog owners who also have horses want nothing more than to have their dogs with them on

Begin working in the general area of horses but not close enough to distract your dog.

Eventually you can start working nearer the horse.

trail rides. The dogs usually end up running three times as far as the horses, so there is no better way to tire out a high-energy canine than this activity. I try to provide my dogs with this fun event a couple of times a week.

Learning to behave around horses is the first step in enjoying the ride along. As big as they are, horses are prey animals and canines are predators, so you will have to overcome your dog's natural instinct to chase, bark, and nip at the horses. Teddy must have very good control and be very well behaved off lead before being introduced to a horse.

It is best to begin the experience on the long leash. As with other distraction training, you will need to begin far enough away from the horses that they don't make a difference in Teddy's responses.

As he proves consistent, move a little closer, gradually increasing the proximity until you are within six feet of the horse. You don't want to allow your dog any closer, because horses move quickly and you may not be fast enough to pull yourself and your dog far enough away to avoid injury.

The safest way of introducing Teddy to horses is for the horse to be in a stall or a fenced-in field. This gives you a barrier. It is far easier to teach your dog to not cross a barrier to investigate a horse than it is to walk up to a horse with no barrier.

A horse in a stall can reach down and push his nose at the dog. This will allow the two animals to greet each

The first year I had my mixed-breed dog, Princess, she was deathly afraid of horses. She would bark at them from the car and run from any horses she came across. The best experience for her was a week we spent on a farm in Augusta County, Virginia. We rented a log home along the Bull Pasture River where horses and cattle roamed freely. Princess knew to remain within the "stay here" area of the house, but she did venture out when we'd walk to the car. Soon after we arrived, the horses came by to say hello. She crawled up to one to sniff it. I rewarded her for being so good about the greeting. She spent the weekend getting to know those horses, always being rewarded when she showed good manners. Now she runs alongside my horse, on our left side, in heel position (when she's able) as we race through the woods.

other. Once Teddy sniffs the horse, he will have an idea of how to react because you will click and reward him when he shows no signs of aggression or fear. If he does begin to bark or jump at the stall door, call him to come to you, then praise him, click, and reward. Have him do a sit-stay at the stall door. Click and reward often for calm behavior. Gradually increase the amount of time between clicks as he becomes more comfortable with the situation.

While you are near the stall, go through an obedience routine with your dog. Treat the horse as just another distraction that Teddy must learn to ignore while working. As your dog begins to relax and perform, give him frequent breaks to investigate the horse. Always reward him for appropriate behavior and redirect him if he gets tense.

Once Teddy is reliable with the horse in a stall or a fenced area, it is time to teach him to work near a horse who is not behind a barrier. Moreover, since horses move around a lot, whether to graze or swat at flies, your dog must behave during this more intense distraction. (Movement is always more distracting to dogs, hence their drive to chase squirrels, cats, and other fast-moving critters.) You can be sure a horse will be moving quickly while on a trail or running cross-country, and not being aware of the movement can be dangerous for the dog. Hounds who run with hunters quickly learn to stay out of the way of the horses' legs.

Always begin this training on a leash. There will always be situations in

Have your dog perform stays near the stall door.

The dog should respond to your commands regardless of your location.

which your rewards are not as great as those the distraction presents. There will be moments when you will need to back up your commands, whether because your dog wants to chase the horse or the horse goes after the dog. It is also safer to have someone holding and walking the horse while you work with Teddy. This will prevent the uncontrollable situation of the horse chasing the dog.

Once Teddy is working well around the horse and has learned to stay away from the horses' legs while paying attention to you, it is time to mount up. Unless you must ride through a high-traffic area to get to the trails, it is best to begin with Teddy off leash, not wearing any training device. Since he already obeys your cues without a leash, he should also respond to your cues from your higher station—on the horse.

The only commands you'll need are come, leave it, and stay here. You want Teddy to remain in the same area as you, to come when called, and not to go after any small creatures you may encounter (such as a skunk!). Otherwise, it's a free run for all. If your dog does not quickly respond to these commands, it is best not to try giving them from the back of a horse just yet—he will be even less likely to listen when you are farther away from his level. When he does listen, praise, click, and drop down a treat. You may need some treats for your horse as well, because he will need to learn to behave with Teddy nearby. Clicker training works wonders with horses, too.

If you must first ride across or along a busy road, you will need to put Teddy on a long leash to ensure that he remains in heeling position as you cross the area. Teddy can learn to heel just as well with you sitting on your horse as he can with

> One time I met a friend for a ride at Hickory Plantation, a Civil War–era property where Robert E. Lee's brother once stayed when he was injured. The property has 1,800 acres with many wide gravel roads, perfect for horse riding and dog running. To get there we had to cross a neighbor's cornfield and then a small highway. I put leashes on both dogs (my friend and I each had one). The dogs heeled with us through the field and across the highway until we reached the plantation land. Once there, I found a large rock for them to stand on while I took off the leashes. On the way back I again had them stand on the rock so that I could connect the leashes for our highway crossing. This allowed them to accompany us to an otherwise difficult place to travel for both horses and dogs. Good training gives you and your dog more opportunities to play together.

you on your own two legs. The parameters might be a bit different, but the criteria are the same. Again, it's basic distraction proofing.

If you are working at this level, Teddy should not need anything more than a regular collar or harness. Attach a leash, have him sit and stay, then mount up. Proceed with the heel commands as normal, keeping in mind that you cannot give the visual cue of stepping forward with your left leg. Your dog must respond well to the verbal cue. When you must stop to cross the street, do not tell your dog to sit; allow him to remain standing, because you may have to move forward quickly. As

Heeling on a leash while you are riding a horse is not difficult to teach.

he remains in place, praise enthusiastically. When you reach a safe stopping zone, click and reward. Do the same for your horse, because it is just as difficult for him to walk alongside a predator as it is for Teddy to walk alongside prey.

When you reach a place where it's safe to allow Teddy off the leash, there are two ways you can do it: from onboard your horse, or by dismounting, taking off the leash, then remounting. Which sounds easier? It all depends upon your animals. I have taught my horse to remain still as my dogs put their front feet up on a log or large rock. I can then reach down, unsnap the leash, and reward them both. Teddy can also learn to step up, as follows:

1. Begin off your horse. In fact, the horse does not need to be anywhere nearby.

2. You can shape the behavior or lure Teddy into it. I find luring to be faster.

3. Put the lure near the rock you want him to stand on. Have Teddy target it. Click and reward.

4. Do this three times, until Teddy is targeting the rock without you having to place the lure near it.

5. Ask for Teddy to step up on the rock or log by luring him there with the reward.

6. Once he is there, click and reward.

7. Repeat three or four times. If he chooses to put all four feet up, no problem. Click and reward.

8. Add the command pop up as you point to the rock or log.

9. Gradually increase the distance you are from the rock or log as you tell him to pop up.

10. Practice having him stand and stay once he is up. Gradually increase the amount of time he remains before the click and reward.

11. You can now do the same exercise from horseback.

Lure your dog to the object.

Shape your dog to stand on the object.

Teach the cue for the command pop up.

Give the command from horseback.

Take the leash on or off the dog while you remain on your horse.

Chapter 7

Click & Trick

Once your dog understands clicker-reward-based training, there is no limit to the things you can teach him to do. How about teaching your dog to fetch you a cold soda from the refrigerator? Fetch the newspaper? Answer the telephone? Help find the children? Or even find your lost keys?

Many dogs are capable of learning these complex behaviors, but each part of the behavior must be broken down into smaller sections for teaching. As you think up new activities, always keep in mind your dog's physical build and attention span. Each has a bearing not only on what the dog can do, but on how quickly each section can be achieved as you train toward the ultimate goal.

For example, while some dogs might be able to fetch the newspaper, there are others who are physically unable to do so. It's a snap for a Labrador Retriever, but a Maltese may be too small. However, there will be plenty of other tricks a toy dog can do that a Lab may be far too big for.

Think about the types of activities your dog naturally enjoys, as well. While a dog who relies greatly on sight can

Bringing your slippers is a time-honored trick.

locate and chase down a moving object, those who rely more on scenting do better retrieving stationary objects. A dog who is agile will be far more likely to do flips and aerial tricks, while a dog with a longer back and short legs will prefer less acrobatic enterprises.

Any dog can learn to jump through hoops.

When training your dog using positive reinforcement, the key word is *positive*. Make sure every moment of your dog's advanced training remains fun and rewarding. This keeps him wanting to offer more behaviors, and many of those behaviors can be turned into rewarding tricks. You just need to be consistent in what behaviors you reward and maintain accurate timing of your click.

Whatever your dog is doing at the moment he hears the click is the behavior he will identify with the command you have given. For example, if your dog is inviting you to play by putting his front end on the floor while raising his hind end and wagging his tail, and you are working to teach him to bow, you must click *as* he performs this behavior. Your dog discovers that if he offers this behavior, he will be rewarded. It is then your job to shape this behavior into an action performed on your request, rather than your dog merely throwing out behaviors for attention.

BASIC TRICKS

There are five basic tricks that, regardless of size or breed, any dog can learn. They are all based on the sit-stay and down-stay commands but can be shaped into other positions as your dog becomes proficient. These tricks are shake, sit up, wave, roll over, and speak.

Shake

Let's begin with shake. The goal is to have your dog sitting, facing you, with his paw in your hand. Before you begin, decide which paw you'd like the dog to lift. You will ask your dog to target the hand opposite the one he rests his paw on, and you'll need to be consistent with the target and "paw rest" hands if you want your dog to learn quickly.

If your dog has the annoying habit of pawing you, this may not be a good trick to teach until he first learns that pawing is not an acceptable behavior. If he does it to gain attention, he must learn a more positive way of doing so, such as sitting and waiting. Once he understands that pawing alone does nothing for him, you can begin to teach shake.

You'll need to break this behavior down into the following components:

Sit-stay.

Sit-stay while shifting his weight to one side.

Sit-stay, lean, and take the weight off one paw.

Sit-stay, slightly lift the paw, then raise it higher and higher with each successive left.

The dog puts his paw in your hand.

Some dogs seem to learn faster than others. While you might be tempted to skip a step or two, this is probably not a good idea. To create a solid foundation for a behavior, you need to build that behavior methodically. There's much that can be lost in translation along the way, and your dog might be responding to a different stimulus than the one you presented, directing him to the wrong final behavior.

For a dog who has already learned basic and advanced obedience through clicker-reward-based training, the shaping will go quickly. Be patient and persistent.

So, using the stages I just described, you teach your dog shake this way.

1. Sit-stay. By this stage your dog should be able to maintain this position off leash, regardless of where you are.

2. Sit-stay while shifting his weight to one side. Have your dog target the hand opposite the one you want him to shake. If you want him to shake with his left paw, bring your target hand to his right side (your left). As your dog follows the target, click and reward.

3. He must turn his head to the side, not just move his nose. Gradually ask him to increase the movement. Click and reward with each successive improvement.

4. Sit-stay, lean, and take the weight off one paw. As your dog turns his head, he'll actually begin leaning in the direction of the target. When you see this, click and reward.

5. Sit-stay, slightly lift the paw. To accomplish this, your dog will have to lean far enough to take the weight off the paw you wish him to raise. The instant you see his paw leave the floor, click and reward. You'll most likely need to remain at this stage for a few repetitions until your dog realizes exactly which behavior is being rewarded.

6. With each successive lift, hold out for a slightly better performance. This means you should click and reward each time your dog lifts his paw a little higher.

7. The dog puts his paw in your hand. Once your dog can lift his paw as high as his shoulders, you can begin shaping him to place it in your hand. Begin with a click and reward when he touches your hand.

Bring your dog's head to the side using targeting.

As he leans, he'll take the weight off the paw on the opposite side.

Gradually request a higher lift with each success.

The final goal, shake.

There are many more tricks you can do that are based on the shake behavior. One is to ask your dog to guess which hand a treat is in by first sniffing and then putting his paw on the hand holding the treat. Another is to choose which treat he'd prefer by placing his paw on the hand holding the preferred treat. Yet another is to shake with either paw—the cue being different hands.

8. Each time you request his paw, make sure you don't click until he has placed more and more of his paw in your hand. Within a short time (two to four repetitions), the paw should be resting in your hand and your dog will be getting loads of praise and rewards. Always reward handsomely when you reach the ultimate goal—shake.

Sit Up

As with shake, this trick is based upon a solid sit-stay. If you have a dog who likes to jump on you for attention, this exercise might be a good compromise. He can rise up halfway, without touching you, and receive a reward. (It's a lot better than full impact with muddy paws.) Plus, he'll be doing it on command, which means your dog will be thinking about how to be good instead of annoying you. Keep in mind that negative attention is still attention, and guiding your dog into a more positive way of getting your attention will reinforce better behavior.

We will need to break down this behavior into increments, as follows:

Sit-stay with the dog's head looking up.

Sit-stay with his head looking up and his weight pushed back onto the haunches.

Sit-stay with slight lift upward.

Sit-stay with gradually more and more upward lift.

Gradually increase the stay time.

So, using these stages, you teach your dog sit up this way.

1. Sit-stay with the dog's head looking up. Use a lure (a treat or a toy) to get your dog to look up. He must look straight up, not at you. When his head and eyes are glued to the target, click and reward. Repeat several times.

2. Sit-stay with his head looking up and his weight pushed back onto the haunches. By the third repetition, he should also be shifting his weight back. Begin using the command, Up (or whatever you wish; just be consistent).

First, get your dog looking up at the visual cue.

Gradually lure him to lift himself higher on cue.

Now add the stay command when he's sitting up.

Another trick that is based on sit up is to rise totally onto the back paws. From there you can teach Teddy to either walk on his hind legs and/or twirl. He can also fetch in this position. I once saw a video of a dog who did a complete retrieve walking solely on his hind legs. Because of basic canine structure this is very difficult to do, so the rewards must be worthy of the task.

3. Sit-stay with slight lift upward. Hold the target just out of reach and give the Up command. This time, reaching upward with his head won't be enough to receive his click. He must push upward, his front feet briefly leaving the floor. The instant you see his front feet leave the floor, click and reward. Repeat this at least two times—three if your dog seems insecure about the exercise.

4. Sit-stay with gradually more and more upward lift. Expect slightly more lift each time you repeat this. Be careful not to click when your dog does less than you had expected; this leads to regression instead of progression. Expect more and you'll get more. Be consistent and you'll enable understanding.

5. Gradually increase the stay time. By the fifth or sixth repetition (or less), your dog should be doing the up exercise: weight on his haunches, both front feet in the air, his nose targeting upward as he balances. This may appear to be a finished exercise, but it isn't. Your dog must learn to remain in place for more than a mere second. Once up, incorporate the stay, gradually increasing the time you expect your dog to hold the up position.

Just as you had built up the time your dog could hold a sit-stay, gradually increase the amount of time on the sit up before he earns his click and reward. However, to encourage his efforts, praise him while he stays. Don't expect more than a ten- to fifteen-second stay because this position is very difficult for your dog to maintain. It is especially difficult for puppies and long-backed breeds, such as Dachshunds, Corgis, and Basset Hounds.

Wave

This trick is an extension of the shake, so before you start, make sure your dog has really learned shake. Then the behavior is broken down into these parts.

Sit-stay and shake.

Move your hand slightly toward yourself and allow your dog to place his paw in it as he reaches out.

Move your hand toward you twice before your dog is allowed to place his paw in your hand.

Gradually move your hand toward you so that Teddy's paws can't reach it.

Add the command wave as your dog reaches for your hand two to three times.

Have your dog reach toward your hand with his paw.

1. Sit-stay and shake. Always begin with something your dog knows well, so he can earn a positive reaction from you. This gets him in the mood to learn. Practice the shake trick a few times, giving your dog lots of clicks and rewards for performing correctly.

2. Ask your dog to shake, then move your hand slightly toward yourself and allow your dog to place his paw in it as he reaches out.

3. Move your hand toward you twice before your dog reaches out to place his paw in your hand. This will mean Teddy must stretch a little further to reach your hand.

4. Gradually move your hand toward you so that Teddy's paw can't reach it. Don't allow him to place his paw in your hand. As he reaches for your hand, his paw will wave in the air. Click and reward.

5. Repeat and make your dog try to reach you twice. As he does so, click and reward.

6. Add the command, Wave as you ask Teddy to reach for your hand two or three times. By now your dog has figured out that something new is happening. The next time you do this exercise, say, Wave instead of Shake. As he moves his paw toward your hand, move your hand slightly up and down. Click and reward as he moves his paw up and down, too.

Each time you do the exercise, request another paw movement; however, don't ask for more than three or four waves. More than that and your dog will become frustrated and might offer another behavior to receive his reward. Each dog has his own behavior threshold, which is the number of repetitions or length of time he will perform an exercise. While this can gradually be increased over time, most dogs have absolute limits that must be respected.

Roll Over

Ready for something different? This trick is based on the down-stay. Any dog is capable of doing the rollover, but some just don't like it because it puts them in a very submissive position. Many dominant and/or insecure dogs may not enjoy this trick. And that's the very reason you should teach the dog to perform it. Not only must your dog learn that he must comply with your commands, but he must also learn to be comfortable exposing his underside.

Don't tell me you wouldn't feel exposed rolling over on your back with someone standing over you! It takes time to accept, but by using the clicker and positive reinforcement, your dog will learn this trick and offer it to you whenever he wants to grab your attention. And who can ignore a dog rolling over in front of them? Certainly not me!

This is a complex behavior and will need to be broken down into several steps. Here's how:

Down-stay.

Down-stay with the dog's head over his shoulder.

Down-stay with the dog's head over his shoulder and the dog lying on his side.

Down-stay with the dog's head moving toward his back.

Down-stay with the dog lying tummy up.

Down-stay with the dog having rolled completely to other side, lying on his side.

The dog rolls all the way over and finishes with a sit or a stand.

Not long ago, I was working on a television commercial for Northern Virginia Electric Cooperative with Xena, a Jack Russell Terrier. Xena has been performing in front of the camera for years. On this particular occasion, she decided to offer a few behaviors along with the ones her owner and I were teaching. One of them was roll over. She was only supposed to do a sit from a down, then turn her head and bark. But she inserted the rollover into her repertoire in the hope of earning her click and reward faster.

Each time we placed her in the down-stay on her mark, she rolled over, just to see if that would earn more treats. (She was getting freeze-dried liver that day, a super-duper treat that she doesn't normally receive.) She was even offering behaviors to earn more rewards between takes! Her owner and I understood what she was doing, and we just laughed (faces turned away from her so she couldn't see us, of course). Who could ignore that huge grin on Xena's face?

Tummy rubs help relax your dog.

While some dogs may require all of these steps to shape the rollover, others may skip a few in the middle. You'll have to see how your dog reacts to this exercise. Some dogs may even need a little help, with you bringing their legs around. As always, click and reward the instant your dog has accomplished something, even if you moved him into position. With the constant positive reinforcement, he will be willing to keep trying even though the action you requested might make him uneasy.

1. Down-stay. Your dog must be comfortable performing a down-stay with you touching him. Most dogs love tummy rubs, and that's the best way of reinforcing a long down-stay. Touch is a great reward.

2. Down-stay with the dog's head over his shoulder. Using a lure or a target stick, lure your dog to move his head over his shoulder. The instant his head turns, click and reward. Repeat, requesting a little more movement each time. Before going on to the next step, your dog should easily be moving his head to his shoulder.

3. Down-stay with the dog's head over his shoulder and the dog lying on his side. As your dog moves his head to his shoulder, he should shift his weight to the same side as his head. This helps him balance the movement. The instant you see his weight shift, click and reward. If he does not shift his weight, help him do so by pressing your hand gently against his hip until he becomes more comfortable. Click and reward as soon as he attains this position.

4. Down-stay with the dog's head moving toward his back. Now that your dog understands how to shift his weight, he can move his head further around. Hold out for his reaching around to his back. The instant he does so, click and reward.

5. Down-stay with the dog lying tummy up. This is the trickiest part of the exercise. Some dogs will resist going onto their back and try to reach around in the other direction to get their reward. If your dog tries to do this, persistently resist and go back a step. Prove to him that his success lies in your direction, not another. You might need to help him onto his back by taking his legs—one front leg, one rear leg—and helping him onto his back. The instant he has accomplished this, whether you put him there or not, click and reward. The next time will be easier, because he'll have a better understanding of what you want.

6. You'll need to pause at this point to make sure that your dog has a full understanding of this step. Click and reward freely when he is able to do this on his own. It is a huge step to take.

Lure your dog's head to his shoulder.

Lying on his side with his head toward his rear.

Tummy up can be turned into another trick—lie still. (It looks a lot like the old "play dead.")

A complete roll to the other side must be rewarded.

7. Down-stay with the dog having rolled completely to other side, lying on his side. When your dog is comfortable lying on his back, it shouldn't be a problem to complete the roll onto the other side. Lure your dog all the way around, then click and reward when he has completed the roll.

8. The dog rolls all the way over and finishes with a sit or a stand. This last step isn't necessary for the trick, but it will prevent your dog from rolling all over the room looking for more rewards. You can get your dog back on his feet by praising him for the roll and then coaxing him back onto his feet. The coax can be done by slapping your legs, clapping your hands, or luring with food or a toy. Regardless of your method, click and reward when your dog has successfully completed the entire behavior.

When your dog is lying tummy up, you can turn this position into another trick—lie still. Just add the stay to the position, gradually requiring him to remain longer before you click to signal success. Once he understands what you want, add your lie still command, pairing it with the action and his reward.

You now have a dog who can roll over, lie still, shake, wave, and sit up. Wow! This repertoire keeps expanding. What's next?

Speak

Every dog can bark, whine, squeal, and growl, so speak can have as many nuances as you have ideas. You can elicit a heavy bark, a whine, or a sneeze with ease. Think of situations in which each will be appropriate. Do you want your dog to let you know when he needs to go out? Do you want your dog to let you know when there is someone near your home? Does your dog have a speaking part in a movie for which he needs to learn his lines?

There are several ways you can elicit the bark you will need to teach your dog to speak on command. One is to get him excited enough to bark. Another is to place him with other dogs who already know speak. A third way is to be ready to capture the behavior in a situation in which he usually barks, then pair the command with the behavior and reward him accordingly.

Regardless of which method you use to teach your dog to speak, you can use the clicker to mark the moment he does what you want. The first two methods will require you to break down the behavior and shape it. The third method will require you to limit the behavior to only those times you request it. This method tends to work well in curing an excessive barker, giving him a more positive outlet for his cacophonous ways.

Speak with Excitement

We'll begin with how to teach speak by getting your dog excited. This should be broken down into very small parts. You must be aware of your dog moving his mouth and not require him to be in any particular position—there are dogs who will begin barking more readily when they are standing and others who prefer to do their barking lying down. The body position can be adjusted after you are successful in teaching your dog to speak.

The amount of activity required to excite a dog depends on the dog. It can be anything from you moving quickly to jumping up and down to using playful vocal expressions. Begin with the minimum and work your way into more excitement, until your dog begins jumping around and moving his mouth. If he starts any type of verbal expression, click and reward. He can sneeze, whine, or grumble—anything at all. Reward immediately, then do it again. As you continue, it will get easier and easier to elicit sound from Teddy. He has learned that the more noise he makes, the more rewarding it can be. If you have other dogs, the two of them might get into a play mode that will make them even more excited, causing more barking.

Once you know what it takes to elicit the bark, begin with that level of excitement and action. Teddy will identify one or several cues, all on his own, as you get him excited enough to bark. You will need to figure out what cue he is responding to. Was it your hands against your ears? You jumping up and down? Running back and forth? You can figure it out by doing just one or two of the actions and seeing if Teddy responds.

Once you discover the body language that he is using as a cue, you can phase out all the other actions and use just that one movement. For example, you begin by jumping up and down. You raise one of your hands to the outside of your ear as you do this. After several repetitions in which Teddy is quickly responding, you can phase out the jumping, leaving the visual cue of your hand to your ear and begin using the verbal cue of speak. Eventually, you'll be able to cue Teddy to speak by either putting your hands to your ear or using the verbal command. You won't need both.

Capture the Word

There are two easy ways to capture this behavior. One is to make it happen through "show and tell" and the other is to do something that you know will make your dog bark. In show and tell, you have your dog near other dogs who know how to bark on command. The excitement and commotion will make Teddy do the same. When he speaks, you click and reward. Until then, you will click and reward the other dog who responds to the command and ignore Teddy. Dogs do not like being left out of dog games. Teddy will eventually join in and discover how much fun it can be to be part of the chorus, as well as how rewarding it is to speak out when given the cue.

Many of us do not have the luxury of already owning or knowing a dog who can speak on command. In this case, you need to do something that will make Teddy speak. Knock on the door, ring the door bell, bark (dogs aren't the only ones who

Dogs learn from one another.

know how to bark). The moment Teddy shows any sign of making noise, click and reward. As he progresses, shape the behavior by clicking as he offers more and more sound.

When he's consistently responding to whatever you're doing, add a command cue, such as your hand behind an ear or saying "speak." Because you are pairing together the current cue (the doorbell, for example) and the new one, it may take a few repetitions to transfer. After about five great responses, stop the old cues of knocking on the door or ringing the bell and use only the verbal and visual cues you want Teddy to learn for speak.

Extinguish the Noise

Nobody likes a big mouth. A dog who barks incessantly at everything is a major annoyance. There may be a zillion reasons why he's so noisy, but he must learn to use his voice at appropriate moments, not when he chooses to get attention or to scare off the sparrows. By teaching Teddy to speak on command, you will be directing him to the appropriate, rewarding moments to use his penchant for vocalizing.

In general, once Teddy learns to speak on command, you can redirect him when he is barking at the wrong moments. Simply redirect him to a rewarding activity, such as chewing on a yummy bone, playing, or doing some obedience work. When he speaks on command, reward with clicks and treats.

Specific breeds are prone to nuisance barking. If Teddy belongs in this group, always be ready to redirect him into a more positive, less annoying behavior.

Yelling at him will only add to his barking fervor. He will need another outlet for all that energy.

You can also teach him a Quiet cue.

1. When Teddy is barking without you requesting it, ignore him or redirect him. (Redirecting will quiet him more quickly.)

2. Click and reward when Teddy has turned his attention to the other activity.

3. When your dog will quickly redirect his attention, add the Quiet cue.

4. The next time Teddy is barking, tell him "Quiet" and redirect him. Click and reward the moment he is quiet.

5. Gradually increase the amount of time between the cue, his reaction, and the click. This will add more *quiet* time to your life.

FUN WITH TOYS

There are *a lot* of tricks you can do with Teddy's toys. I'll cover a few of the starter basics here, but feel free to run with it. We'll begin by teaching Teddy to target three very different toys, recognizing them by name. With this skill you can teach him to go find a specific toy, retrieve that toy, and take the toy to a specific location. This can evolve into the behavior-chaining games (games that string together several skills) of Find and Seek, Go and Bring, or Take and Leave. Not only will this offer Teddy some great mental stimulation, but it can also teach him to be useful as a search and rescue dog, therapy dog, or media hound. His working abilities will be incredible.

Target a Named Toy

We begin this exercise where we started with the targeting process. Back in chapter 2, we had Teddy targeting toys, hands, and the target stick. To teach Teddy to target a specific toy, you need to name the toy as you tell him "touch."

1. Present the toy, and point to it with the target stick.

2. Tell Teddy, "touch."

3. The moment Teddy touches the stick and/or toy, click and reward.

4. Repeat this four times, allowing Teddy to touch the toy at will.

5. The fifth time, name the toy as Teddy touches it. For example, ball or duck or rope.

6. Repeat three or four times, clicking and rewarding each time.

7. Now name the toy and tell Teddy to touch it without using the target stick: "Teddy, touch ball." You may need to wait a few moments as Teddy works out the situation. You might get some behaviors you didn't ask for,

such as sitting and speaking, or lying down. You must ignore this and do not laugh. Laughing is a positive response for doing something you did not ask for and will encourage Teddy to continue. Merely wait. Be patient.

8. Teddy will eventually touch the toy. Give him a jackpot! Click, then lots of rewards and petting.

9. Repeat this three or four times, giving the verbal cue of "touch [name of toy here]," and clicking and rewarding the instant he does so.

Begin by using the target stick to get the dog to touch the toy.

Teddy now knows how to touch this specific toy. Next, you need to teach him the names of two other toys. Do the same exercise, but use a different toy. When you are sure he has learned the name of the toy, start again with a third toy.

Now Teddy is quickly touching each of the three toys when you name it. But each toy has been presented alone to him. It's time to make this more difficult by teaching him to touch the toy you name when all three are present.

1. Place two toys near one another on the floor.

2. Direct Teddy to touch one of them.

3. If he touches the correct one, click and reward. If not, wait until he does. Again, he might do a few things to get your attention, such as sit, speak, lie down, or roll over. Ignore him until he touches the toy you named. He should know the name of the toy. He may simply be confused about choosing between two toys.

4. Once Teddy is reliable on touching one particular toy, ask him to touch the other toy.

5. Click and reward only when he touches the toy you asked for.

6. Repeat three or four times.

7. Now you can interchange the toy you want him to touch. Vary the one you ask for to ensure he recognizes the toys by name.

Use the target stick to direct your dog to choose the toy you named.

8. As Teddy becomes reliable touching only the named toy, add the third toy.

9. Ask him to touch only this third toy for three or four repetitions.

10. When he is reliable, start mixing up the toy targets.

Teddy can now discern the names of his toys and touch the one you request. Smart dog!

Retrieve a Toy

If Teddy naturally loves to retrieve, this will be easy. If he doesn't, you will first need to teach him some basic retrieving before you can work on retrieving a specific toy on cue. Break down the retrieve this way.

1. Begin with targeting his favorite toy.

2. When he is reliably touching the toy, ask for a little more: He must put his mouth on it.

3. Now he must pick it up in his mouth before he gets his click and reward.

4. He must pick it up and carry it a short distance.

5. Gradually increase the distance until he has brought the toy to you.

6. When he is going to get the toy and bringing it to you, he must put it in your hand.

As Teddy learns to bring you the toy, begin throwing it short distances for him to retrieve. Dogs enjoy this more active retrieving game. Remember that movement triggers their prey drive and a moving toy makes the dog want to give chase.

Gradually increase the criteria until Teddy is bringing you the toy.

If, at any time, Teddy looks at you with a bewildered expression and does not perform as you requested, back up to where he was performing reliably. Also, keep in mind that his attention span may not be able to handle a long training session, so give him frequent breaks. It is just as important to rest the mind as it is to challenge it.

Find It

Now it's time for a really fun game, Find It. This is a great exercise when you're preparing a dog for search and rescue or assistance dog work. It is also plain all-around fun for both you and Teddy. Begin by teaching your dog to find specific toys; then he can learn to find specific people.

1. Put Teddy in a stay and place the toy next to a large object, such as a couch, or partially around a corner, so that he can see only a small part of the toy. Cue Teddy to fetch the toy. Click and treat when he arrives.

2. Next time, hide more of the toy. Send your dog to fetch it. Click and reward when he does.

3. When you're sure your dog understands, hide the toy in a totally different place. Not someplace difficult—just out of Teddy's sight. Give him the cue to fetch it. Click and reward when he returns with the toy.

4. When you are sure Teddy is totally clear that his task is to find the toy, switch to another toy. Repeat steps 1 through 3, practicing until you are sure he is equally comfortable finding and retrieving both items.

Partially hide the toy before sending your dog to retrieve it.

5. Now hide two toys. When you give Teddy the cue Find It, you must also name the toy you wish him to retrieve. You will need to use several cues, such as "find ball, Fetch." Or simply, "find ball." (Teddy already knows he must bring you the ball to receive the click and treat.)

If Teddy shows up with the wrong toy, don't correct him. Give him the Keep Going cue by not responding with the click and treat when he returns holding the wrong item. He might try some behaviors to draw your attention to the fact that he returned with something, even if it wasn't what you asked for. Don't give in, and don't laugh either (at least not in front of him), because that will reinforce the behavior. If you laugh, he'll know he made you happy and will keep doing the same thing. So be cool. Maintain the criteria you set. Give Teddy no response until he returns to you with the item you requested. The instant he does, click and give him loads of praise and a couple of treats. Celebrate! Teddy had to use a lot of brainpower to do this trick.

When your dog is reliably identifying and retrieving one of the two toys, switch gears and ask for the other one. As he shows his ability to remember the names of the toys, you can add more toys to the game. The number of items you can use is endless, as Teddy can learn the names of anything.

How about having your dog learn the names of your family members? This can be a great family game as you have Teddy go from one to the other. You can start with the Round Robin game, in which your dog comes to each person who calls him. Your family members sit all around the room. Start with one family member calling Teddy to come. He gets his click and reward, then that person points to someone else and says, "go to Harry [put a family member's name here]." Harry then immediately calls Teddy to come. Teddy will receive a click and reward each time he goes to the right person, and through repetition he'll learn everyone's name. When he is very reliable at going to the correct person, the come command will no longer be needed. The person sending the dog can just give the verbal cue "go to Harry." When Teddy arrives, Harry clicks and treats.

Make this game a little more challenging by having all the family members go to different rooms. You can have Teddy search the house for the person who is named. You don't need a specific breed of dog that is intended for this work; a toy dog can find his family members as easily as a scenting dog. It's all in the positive training that offers fun for everyone.

I have had the pleasure of working with an Australian Shepherd who remembers everyone's name, once he is *formally* introduced to a person. His human companion simply says, "This is [whomever]" and tells him to say hi. After this initial introduction, he never forgets a name.

Teddy, the actual namesake for the dog in this book, has been taught to open the refrigerator and bring his human companion what we ask for. More than once he has shown up with items he has removed from the refrigerator without being asked. Granted, he didn't totally steal them by taking them to his bed and eating them. He merely made the suggestion by presenting them to his human companion. Luckily, Teddy has good manners. But not all dogs will control themselves to this extent when it comes to a food they really value.

DOORS AREN'T BARRIERS

Think hard before you teach your dog to open and close doors. Do you really want Teddy to be able to do this? You can be sure he will be doing it even when you don't give him the cue. Once you have developed a dog who thinks on this level, he will often use his knowledge to his own advantage. You may need to start locking the doors, especially if you've taught him to open the refrigerator.

Be sure to choose just one door when you start and be consistent in using only that particular door. I suggest it be a bedroom door, because this will present fewer problems than, say, a bathroom door or a door that leads outside. I'd much rather have Teddy enter my bedroom than to come into the bathroom or help himself to a neighborhood romp.

There are many parts to this trick, and each must be taught separately before you can expect Teddy to put it all together and perform the entire sequence. Here are the skills your dog must learn.

1. Go to the door.
2. Push his nose into the slightly open door.
3. Push at the door enough to open it.
4. Go through the door to the other side.
5. Retrieve an item from the other side.
6. Close the door.
7. Bring the item to you.
8. Give the item to you.

So, there are at least eight different behaviors Teddy must learn. Each behavior will need to be broken down even further. This is a complex trick!

Let's begin with the behaviors Teddy already knows. He can retrieve a requested item and he can target anything. So nosing something and fetching something are not new to him. Now we need to teach the behaviors that are new: opening and closing doors.

Use the target stick to get
Teddy to touch the door.

You must teach Teddy to
push his nose between the
door and frame.

Bringing the item to you is a
retrieve—which he already
knows.

Open the Door

At first you will need to facilitate this by leaving the door partially open. Turning a knob or pushing against a latch is a very difficult behavior for a dog, and this is not the time to introduce it. Besides, do you really want Teddy to be able to do this? I surely wouldn't. My dogs would be following me everywhere, instead of remaining safely at home when I can't take them with me.

There are ways to teach your dog to pull on a loop of rope or a towel to open a refrigerator or cupboard, but I don't suggest you teach him to undo latches or turn knobs.

Let's begin by teaching Teddy to open the door.

1. Leave the door open a crack.

2. Teach Teddy to target the door, placing his nose against the open edge.
   Since you previously taught him to target by saying "touch," you need to

add another cue that specifically means "push the door open." I suggest the verbal cue "Teddy, open door." As always, add the cue when the behavior is a sure thing. That way you are building on success instead of forcing failure.

3. Shape his responses until he is pushing his nose between the open door and the frame.

4. With each success, request more of a push action before his click and reward.

When the door is open wide enough for him to move through, you have accomplished this step. You can test Teddy's abilities by placing a favorite toy on the other side of the door. Leave the door open just enough for him to push through with his nose. Cue him to retrieve the toy through the door by saying, "Teddy, open door, fetch ball." If your dog can do this, he's halfway there—and another celebration is in order. This is also a very complicated chain of behaviors and requires a lot of canine brainpower.

To have your dog open something that requires pulling rather than pushing, you'll need to teach him to grab a towel or rope that you have attached to the handle. Let's say you want Teddy to open the refrigerator and fetch you a soda. Prepare for this trick by tying a loop of thick rope (maybe one of his rope pull toys) to the refrigerator handle. He already knows what to do with his rope pull, so the transfer will not be difficult. Using another object, such as a towel (which he will most likely be inhibited to pull because it isn't one of his own toys), will add more learning time to the behavior.

1. Begin by having Teddy target the rope pull hanging from the refrigerator door.

2. Next, have him put his mouth on the rope.

3. When Teddy is successfully grabbing the rope, he must pull at it to receive his click and treat.

4. Gradually shape Teddy into pulling harder, until he actually opens the refrigerator.

At this point you can add a cue to fetch any item you have already taught him the word for. Just be sure the package of hotdogs is well out of his reach, or he might help himself to his own reward.

I once had a very clever cat named Crockett who was very adept at turning doorknobs. This was a self-taught behavior, and he was always rewarded with either being in my presence or letting himself outside. I never had any privacy from him, and it did prove dangerous when he insisted on going outside. I therefore highly recommend that Teddy's training remain within the limits of safety.

Targeting the rope should be easy by now.

Teddy must pull hard enough to open the refrigerator door.

Close the Door

This is also a behavior that needs to be shaped. It is quite easy, though, because pushing into a door is a more natural behavior than squeezing between the door and the frame. In fact, as Teddy learns to target the door, he'll tend to push against it.

1. Begin working on targeting the door.
2. Open the door slightly, and repeat the touch cue.
3. When Teddy pokes his nose at the door, there's a good chance it will move. As it does, click and treat.
4. Open the door a little more. Repeat step 3, requiring Teddy to push a little harder for his reward.
5. As Teddy closes the door each successive inch, gradually increase how much you leave it open.
6. When he is adept at closing the door, add the command "Teddy close door."

Now we have all the elements of the behavior. Bring them all together by backchaining. Don't set Teddy up for failure by suddenly asking for everything at once.

Teddy must close the door to complete the sequence.

Through back-chaining you can decrease the number of cues you need for the exercise by teaching your dog the specific pattern.

We'll begin with fetching the requested item through an already open door. When your dog brings it to you, click and treat. Next, close the door until it is ajar. Tell Teddy, "open door and fetch [insert the item name here]." With that successfully accomplished, ask Teddy, "open door, fetch item, close door." Don't be afraid to remind him to close the door (as he's coming through), because his mind will be set on retrieving the object. However, don't click and treat until the entire sequence has been completed.

If at any time Teddy is showing confusion by either hesitating or not performing, go back a bit and work on the specific behaviors that are giving him trouble, until he more clearly understands what you want. At this point in training it's very unlikely that Teddy is being stubborn. He already has a huge work drive and merely wishes to do what you ask. If something isn't clear, he will hesitate. Guide him through with a positive attitude and many rewards.

Chapter 8

Smile, Don't Growl!

Wouldn't it be a perfect world if all dogs were born and raised in a good family environment and knew nothing but love and clear communication? Unfortunately, this isn't the case. Reality dictates that while some dogs have the benefits of good breeding and careful rearing, most do not. In fact, most dogs are the result of either poorly planned or accidental conception. In such situations, little to no thought has been given to behavioral outcomes.

While responsible breeders look at all the facets (and consequences) of a particular pairing, a commercial breeder, or a casual one, merely produces dogs to sell as registered purebreds without taking into consideration the parents' health and behaviors. Then there are the neighborhood Don Juan dogs whose owners do not give a second thought to neutering and/or spaying to prevent unwanted litters, creating mixed-breed dogs who end up in shelters more often than in good homes. And there are the feral dogs, common throughout the country in every environment from urban to rural. Members of the canine family are so adaptable that even the wild coyotes have learned how to successfully exist in suburbia—a noticeable nuisance although they are rarely seen.

There are as many different canine personalities as there are human ones, so we can rarely place a label on a dog's overall propensity for specific behaviors. Granted, certain breeds were created for specific tasks, and we can state, for example, that a terrier will tend to be tenacious, a herding dog will try to gather, and a dog of a sporting breed will always be on the lookout for a good hunt. But we cannot say that one specific breed is more likely to be aggressive than another.

Unfortunately, the current trend of banning certain breeds is causing people to view these breeds in a very negative way, when it is not the *breed* that has caused problems, but individual dog *owners* who have shown either negligence or criminal behavior in training the poor creature to be aggressive.

141

Recently I was looking into home insurance policies and I noticed that one of the questions on the application asked if I owned a purebred or mixes of Pit Bulls, Staffordshire Bull Terriers, Rottweillers, Doberman Pinschers, German Shepherds, or Bulldogs. I suppose that if I had answered yes, the rate quotes would either be very high or I would not even be offered coverage.

Having worked with all those breeds for the past thirty years, I have yet to feel afraid of them solely for what they are. In fact, most of the dogs of these breeds that I've met have been sweet to a fault and wanted only to communicate with their human companions and learn about their environment. On the other hand, many of the toy breeds I've dealt with, as well as some of the sporting breeds, have had aggression issues. I mention this only to point out that aggression is not necessarily a breed-related behavior, but more directly a result of poor rearing.

A good friend of mine, Alice DeGroot, DVM, once told me, "A dog does not bite without a reason."

This chapter is intended to help you recognize the reasons behind aggressive behavior and give you a general idea of how to solve any issues you uncover, using positive reinforcement. Because aggression begets aggression, the best cure is to first understand why the dog is displaying this behavior, and then to formulate a behavior modification program.

This chapter will not give you all the tools you need to overcome aggression in your dog. For that you must consult a professional dog trainer who is well versed in working with canine aggression. It takes a professional with years of experience to recognize all the various types of aggression, identify their underlying behavioral patterns, and deal with the problem.

I will start out by explaining how to recognize potential aggression by understanding calming signals. These are behaviors dogs will display when they are entering a potentially stressful situation in which they either perceive or will initiate aggression. Appropriate reaction on your part to these signals can both avert and defuse incidents of aggression. A professional trainer can quickly recognize these signals and be prepared for an appropriate reaction to prevent and/or defuse aggressive displays.

Once I discuss these calming signals and how they can be used to redirect aggression into amiable behavior, I'll break down each type of aggression and discuss ways of redirecting Teddy. Because aggression arises as a result of many different environmental factors, we need to assess both the environment in which the dog was raised and the one in which he now lives.

CALMING SIGNALS

Dogs communicate using body language, verbal sounds, and pheromones (scent). Recognizing specific patterns of communication before an aggressive episode will help you identify when this behavior is being the initiated and give you a starting

In dog language, licking is a calming signal.

point to redirect Teddy into a more positive reaction.

A number of clear signals say "calm down" in canine language. These are licking, sniffing, sitting or lying down, averting the gaze, walking slowly around another in an arc instead of head-on, yawning, and shaking off. Another dog will understand that the dog displaying the calming signal doesn't want a confrontation. Thus, a dog who is communicating this way should be rewarded for doing so.

Rewarding your dog when he displays these signals will encourage him to remain calm. Not recognizing his heightened tension until he shows aggression will leave you trying to address a difficult behavior in a negative manner.

As you approach someone or something that might frighten or incite your dog, observe his behavior. When you first notice him making a calming signal, click and reward him for it. Work with him a bit in that area, redirecting his attention to obedience exercises or tricks. When he is no longer displaying the calming signals, go a little closer to the thing(s) that triggered his behavior. As with any distraction proofing, you will gradually shape Teddy's behavior by first recognizing what might initiate a fear or aggressive response and then diffusing the situation by redirection.

The easiest way to redirect the dog is to use a head halter, so that instead of punishing him by inflicting pain or psychological trauma, you are merely redirecting his attention to you by turning, stopping often, and requesting other behaviors. The turns you do should gradually bring you closer to the object of Teddy's tension by circling around into that particular space.

Of course, if the object is another dog, he most likely won't remain in place until Teddy learns to control himself. The other dog will move around, possibly responding to Teddy by barking or lunging, wanting either to play or to remove your dog from his territory. In this situation, Teddy will most likely ignore your treats regardless of

Redirect your dog by turning in the opposite direction.

their value, becoming further incited into a reciprocal aggressive response. You will need both hands to work the leash, so you won't be able to properly use your clicker in this situation. The head halter will give you the leverage and control you will need to teach your dog to respond to you instead of to the other dog. When you regain Teddy's attention, take the clicker in your hand again and click it so you can mark the moment he behaves the way you want him to.

Using these methods will not cure Teddy's problem in one training session. After all, it took more than five minutes to develop the aggressive behavior in the first place. It might take months to extinguish it. Take your time and build on the small successes. Each time you work with Teddy have a very small goal in mind— say getting only five feet closer to the thing that raises his hackles. You won't have success if you are constantly struggling with Teddy as you get closer to the object, animal, or person faster than he can calmly handle it.

TYPES OF AGGRESSION

Aggression arises out of frustration and lack of communication. Opening up the communication process takes away the need for aggressive behavior.

Obedience training alone helps cure most of the aggression issues I will cover in this section. Obedience training teaches dogs that pleasant things happen when they pay attention and defer to their human companions, while either nothing or something aversive happens when they misbehave by displaying aggression.

Showing aggression to a dog who is displaying it will only heighten the episode, so your job is to redirect your dog's attention to something with positive associations. Obedience training does just that—redirecting the dog into performing for you because Teddy realizes that the work is fun and he learns more about his environment in the process, reducing the need to communicate using aggressive tactics.

Aggressive behavior manifests itself in different ways. I'll explain each type briefly, and then we will look at them in more detail.

- **Territorial aggression.** The dog displays protectiveness of a specific location. This type of behavior is seen when someone or something enters the dog's home territory. The dog will alert to the intruder and if the intruder does not heed that warning, aggression ensues.

- **Fear aggression.** The dog displays protectiveness of himself. The behavior is often seen in a dog who feels cornered. He has no other recourse but to display aggression. Fear aggression also means the dog is not secure in his environment.

- **Possessive aggression.** The dog displays protectiveness of specific objects. This might occur with a particular toy that has a very high value to the dog, or when someone approaches the dog's food bowl or bed.

- **Maternal aggression.** This is when a mother dog protects her babies. Maternal aggression is more common in wild, unsocialized dogs or between dogs and other animals than with mother dogs and their people. It is natural for a mother dog to be protective, and the behavior, if minimal, can be allowed provided it is not displayed toward humans. If you have more dogs or other types of pets in the household, a mother dog may feel she must keep them away from her litter for the safety of her pups. This also teaches the other animals to "tread lightly" around the puppies.

- **Redirected aggression.** This happens when the dog cannot reach the specific target that has caused his aggression, and he therefore directs his aggression on the nearest living thing or even an object.

- **Aggression with a physical cause.** This occurs either because the dog has a medical condition that affects his behavior, or because he is in pain and is responding instinctively. In this situation, the dog has no control over his outbursts. The cause may be a physical dysfunction such as a brain tumor, thyroid imbalance, or diabetes. Or he may have chronic pain (such as from arthritis or hip dysplasia) or an injury. Sometimes medications can control the problem.

- **Overt aggression.** In this situation, the dog is genetically inclined to be aggressive without a specific reason. In the thirty years I have been a professional animal trainer, I have seen this behavior in two dogs. One was a Rottweiler puppy and the other was a Siberian Husky. Both dogs came from questionable heritage (they were bred by large commercial breeders—puppy mills) where the behavior and genetics of the parents weren't considered before breeding.

Territorial Aggression

This is usually displayed when one dog sees another dog or person approaching his home. The dog tries to make himself look bigger by raising the fur along his spine, prancing high on his toes, holding his tail and head high and stiff with his ears perked forward, and usually barking at the intruder. Teddy is clearly saying, "You have entered my territory; I am in charge."

While it is nice to have a dog who alerts you to intruders (after all, that was one of their key jobs when dogs were first domesticated), territorial behavior can become an issue when Teddy cannot be turned off. Ultimately, it is your decision, not the dog's, whether to allow someone into your home. Teddy must learn the "enough" or "quiet" command and respond accordingly.

For a dog who gets out of control when you have visitors or another dog comes onto your property, you can use positive reinforcement training (that is, the clicker) to redirect the dog to an appropriate response. You'll need to use a head halter, as this will give you the upper hand in redirecting Teddy the instant he shows interest in the intruder. For example, suppose Teddy gets all worked up whenever he sees a dog passing by his house. He has pulled down curtains, scratched doors and flooring, and flung himself at the door trying to get out. With a head halter you can make Teddy sit and stay while the other dog is walking by, or redirect him into another behavior altogether and, through pattern training, teach him an entirely new response.

The best way to retrain Teddy in this situation is to set things up so a friend walks by with a dog or rings your doorbell at a prearranged time. Here's an example:

1. Teddy sees or hears another dog or the doorbell rings.
2. You squeak a toy or ring a bell.
3. The second Teddy responds to the noise you make, click and reward.
4. Gradually increase the amount of time Teddy must maintain his attention on you before he gets the click and treat.

If Teddy is more interested in the intruder than in the sound you are making, turn him away from the door by using the head halter. When you turn his head away from the focus of his attention, he must also move away. His attention will be diverted from the intruder to you. As he shifts his focus, click and reward.

After Teddy has shifted his focus a few times to the sound you make, add the "enough" or "quiet" cue just before you make the sound to get his attention. This command tells him he is to display more appropriate behavior; it's your calming signal to him.

Some dogs can get extremely worked up over the presence of an intruder. In these situations it would be prudent to consult with a professional dog trainer or behaviorist.

Fear Aggression

This is most common in dogs who have not had proper socialization, been victims of abuse or neglect, or lived in several homes without developing any sense of home territory. All dogs need to feel *at home*. Without this, fear and anxiety can arise.

A dog who is fear aggressive will usually first try to escape a fearful situation. If he is unable to escape, he will bite. Some dogs will growl first, while others won't give any warning. A fear bite is rarely deep, as it is not meant to injure but to warn.

Fear aggression is a learned response. Either the dog discovered that he could get out of a frightening situation by showing this behavior, or he was taught that it was appropriate by being rewarded (often inadvertently) when he displayed the behavior.

When a dog is backing up, growling, and showing his teeth, with his body held low, his tail tucked under his belly, and his neck stretched forward, he is feeling

I've seen many dogs learn to fear strangers because their owners coddled and cooed to them whenever someone approached. This led to a more prominent display of fear aggression and even more coddling (which is a reward) from their people.

One example that comes to mind is a Golden Retriever named Mikie. He was a rescue dog and moved into his new home at just over 1 year old. Before his placement he had shown no aggression at any time. He shared his foster home with five other dogs and two adults.

A few months after he was placed, I received a call from his new owners, who were frantic that they would have to give him up because he had started biting the children's friends and threatening the visiting children's parents when they were ready to go home. Mikie had not yet broken anyone's skin (having done all his nipping from behind on the children's rear ends), but it was still very scary to the children to be chased and nipped. It was equally scary to the parents of the visiting youngsters to be threatened at the front door.

As soon as I walked into Mikie's house, I saw that his aggressive behavior was being reinforced. When Mikie growled and barked at me, his owners soothed him in a soft voice and stroked his coat. Their idea was to calm him, but, since this is a form of positive reinforcement, they had been teaching him that his behavior was appropriate and would earn him rewards.

We began a program of basic obedience training and behavior modification, and Mikie soon learned how to earn positive attention for appropriate behavior and how to control both his fear and his territorial aggression by being redirected to an acceptable behavior. Now he works well off leash in and around his home and sits at the door when people walk in and out.

Dogs seek rewards, and if they are rewarded for aggressive behavior, they will be aggressive. If this behavior is allowed to continue, it will cross over into other situations, as well.

cornered. It is best not to approach this dog, because he will lash out if he sees no exit from the situation. Always offer an alternative; allow him to slowly get used to a new situation or person and don't force the issue. Let him come to you. Reward each small step and soon he'll overcome his fear—replaced with the knowledge that you bring *good* things.

With fear aggression in particular, you must discover the reason for the behavior. Is Teddy afraid of people? Dogs? Specific objects? What about a specific sound? Take the time to observe your dog and learn what frightens him and why.

The only way to overcome his fear reaction is to prove to Teddy that there's nothing to be afraid of. As you progress in obedience training and distraction proofing, you are teaching your dog to take his cues from you—to respond to your commands regardless of what is going on around him. This builds his confidence in himself and his family, which helps him relax at home and when he is out with you.

When you see any type of fear reaction, redirect Teddy to something with which he is familiar. (As with the other types of aggression, it is best to have a head halter on your dog. This will avoid any potentially hazardous situations, because Teddy is under your direct control.) For example, suppose he sees a person who reminds him of someone who had abused him. He is growling, crouching, and holding his ears flat against his head. If you are heeling with him, turn in the opposite direction and refocus his attention on you using praise and obedience exercises. He won't be able to think about the scary person any more because he must concentrate on you. As his thoughts transfer to something positive, he will eventually associate formerly scary things with new, pleasant experiences.

Teddy will also learn to trust you as his pack leader and take his cues from you. If you don't respond to what he might think is threatening, then there will be no reason for him to do so either. Rewarding a fear reaction in any way builds on the fear. Trust and a positive outcome extinguishes the fear.

Possessive Aggression

Let's say Teddy finds a bone while you are walking him. You reach down to take the icky thing out of his mouth and he growls at you. You continue to reach for the bone and Teddy bites you. The bite may not be deep, but it hurts just the same.

This is possessive aggression. Teddy can be possessive about food, toys, his bed, or even people. The bite is normally preceded by an overall stiffness in the dog's body and a warning growl. After the first bite, the person is sufficiently intimidated into not risking another one and refrains from taking the bone out of Teddy's mouth. Teddy has just learned how to control his environment. Now, whenever he growls he gets what he wants.

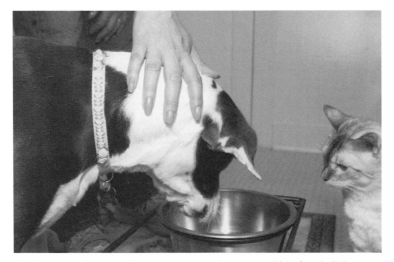

An insecure dog can become aggressive around his food dish.

Possessive aggression is a learned response. It can be a form of dominant aggression. (For more about dominant aggression, see page 156.) It can also occur if a dog is very insecure with his place in the household. The problem is commonly seen in dogs who have been rescued or have recently moved into a new home.

The best way to redirect Teddy to appropriate responses depends on the object of his obsession. Sometimes it is possible to simply remove the object from Teddy's environment or take it away from him. But there are many situations where this will not work. For example, suppose Teddy finds things while you are walking him that you don't want him to have. In an urban or suburban environment, people tend to drop cigarette butts, food wrappers, and other edible "delicacies." Other animals leave their feces about, as well.

Dogs are naturally inquisitive about new scents. The more of these objects you come across, the more often you are taking them from Teddy's mouth. Each time he becomes aroused, because, as he sees it, a food source is being confiscated. If the food is of really high value, such as a meat bone, he might not be willing to allow you to take it from him.

In this type of situation, I recommend using a head halter because Teddy will then be more likely to pay attention to you instead of sniffing the ground while you walk. The head halter offers a humane way of redirecting Teddy, giving you plenty of opportunity to click and reward as he focuses on you. Since this is far more positive than constantly confronting him, he will eventually learn to ignore the trash distraction, the same way he would during any distraction-proofing exercise.

Another approach is to replace an *inappropriate* thing with an *appropriate* thing. The appropriate thing, however, will have to be of much higher value that the inappropriate thing, and it can be tough to compete with a meat bone. You must also make sure you aren't encouraging Teddy to be possessive by rewarding him for aggressive behavior with something even better than the object he's obsessing about. To do that, Teddy must perform a task correctly before he gets the appropriate thing. Something as simple as a sit will do. (Of course, if you want Teddy to understand what he must do to earn the higher-value object, the first step is obedience training. Your dog can't sit on command if he has never learned the command.)

Begin this exchange process by making sure you have your clicker and a high-value reward (freeze-dried liver, hot dog, cheese, steak, or whatever Teddy *really* values). Also make sure Teddy is wearing his head halter, because this gives you the most control of the situation.

1. Allow Teddy to pick up something he normally obsesses over.

2. Show him the higher value reward.

3. The moment he shows interest in the reward, click and give it to him.
   Because he must drop the other object to retrieve his reward, he is learning that you always offer better alternatives. Why should he bother obsessing? Yes, dogs do reason this way. They will always go for the most rewarding situation.

Try different objects to lure Teddy away from the object he is obsessed with.

4. The next time, require Teddy to actually drop the object before you click and give him the reward. Be patient. It may take a little time if the obsessive behavior is self-rewarding. Sometimes nothing can be of a higher value than what Teddy currently has in his mouth, but if you observe him long enough you will see something that draws his attention away. Use whatever that might be as a reward the next time you attempt this exercise.

5. Play a switch game with him. I call this the take-hold-drop game. When you are teaching a dog to retrieve, you shape his behavior of picking up a toy and bringing it to you; you can do the same thing with the object of Teddy's obsession, teaching him to take it, hold it, then drop it on command. This way the object becomes more fun, because it is shared with you and a positive interaction results. Not only will Teddy more readily give up the object without a single snarl, but he will also take it on your command. The possessive aggression has been turned into a constructive game in which you have ultimate control.

When playing the take-hold-drop game, at first don't allow the dog to completely have the toy—you hold one end. Go through the take-hold-drop routine, with a click at the end followed by a reward. When Teddy can hold the object with you and show no possessive behavior, allow him to hold it on his own. If this goes well, gradually increase the amount of time he has possession of it before you tell him to drop it.

A dog who has been raised without appropriate socialization might become possessive about his meals. You also often see this in a "new family" situation: One person had a dog for years, then moves in with another person. The dog enjoyed having

Hold one end of the bone as you allow your dog to hold the other end.

the person all to himself and is not easily willing to both share the person and lower himself in the pack hierarchy, so the dog becomes possessive about specific things such as his bed and/or food dish as a kind of redirected possessive aggression.

Everyone in the household—not just the one toward whom the dog is being aggressive—must address this problem. The person who is clearly receiving respect from the dog must also be consistent in their responses to the dog's aggressive behavior. The behavior cannot be reinforced in any way.

The person who first owned the dog must make sure the dog obeys on one command, regardless of distractions. If this means returning to the basic obedience exercises, do so. This will put the dog in the correct frame of mind to listen when told to do something.

The person who is being targeted by the dog needs to overcome any fear or hesitancy. This is sometimes difficult, but by working with the dog on routine obedience, the communication gap can be bridged and all parties will cooperate.

While basic obedience is being reinforced, try changing the environment during meals. Move Teddy's dish to a new area for each meal. This way he cannot become obsessive about a specific location. The person who is being targeted by Teddy during mealtimes should also be the one to do the following exercise at every meal.

1. Hold the dog's food dish.
2. Tell Teddy to sit. When he does, click and give him a bit of his food.
3. Feed Teddy his entire meal this way. Do not allow Teddy free access to this food until the possessiveness is resolved.
4. After a week, allow Teddy to eat out of his bowl as the person holds the bowl off the floor. However, he cannot have the entire meal right away. It should be given in parts, as a reward for each successful response to a command. As he relaxes into eating without being aggressive, the person can reduce the number of behaviors Teddy must perform while eating.
5. When Teddy is eating his entire meal without showing a stiff body, making growly noises, or lifting his lips, the food dish can be placed on the floor or on a raised feeder. The person should still remain near, praising and petting Teddy as he eats without showing aggression.

When Teddy realizes that all the people in his family are reward dispensers, he'll see that behaving as requested earns him food, while aggression removes his food. The possessiveness should disappear.

Make your dog work for every bite of his meal.

Hold the bowl as the dog eats.

Maternal Aggression

This usually occurs only when a mother dog is protecting her pups and when she doesn't trust the person approaching them. Because most breeders handle all their dogs regularly, people who spend time with the mother and pups are rarely bitten or threatened. In the wild, however, this would be another story. Maternal aggression can also occur if a mother dog doesn't trust the person approaching because she doesn't know them, or because of past neglect or abuse.

The dog will normally threaten before biting. She will growl, lunge, and/or show her teeth. Some might also show fear in their body language, while others try to make themselves appear more fearsome by looking larger. If the intruder is human, the dog is more apt to appear fearful. If the intruder is canine or another type of animal, the dog might appear more dominating.

In a wolf pack, there is only one breeding pair at any given time and the entire clan is involved in raising the puppies. A domestic dog pack is different, though, and the puppies are at risk from all the other dogs in the pack. Therefore, the mother dog will tend to show aggression first and ask questions later. The pack quickly learns to respect her. Even if the mother dog lives with a professional breeder, she might change her behavior toward her siblings or packmates while she is raising her young. Once the pups are weaned and/or in their new homes, she'll return to being less formidable and more interactive with the pack.

Maternal aggression is instinctive. Dogs have a natural tendency to protect their young. Challenging this is dangerous because the dog will rarely back down. The only cure is prevention. The mother dog must be trained and learn to trust her human companions before she is ever bred. This is essential to preventing both stress and dangerous situations during what should be a very pleasant event.

Redirected Aggression

This occurs when a dog cannot behave aggressively toward the object of his anger and, instead, he directs his aggression to the closest living thing or object. This reaction is likely when two or more dogs in a group become overly excited by another animal or person and begin to go after each other. Because they are completely overpowered by their territorial emotions, these fights can often be disastrous and one or more dogs winds up being severely injured.

One of my clients added a rescued Chow Chow named Missy to her household of one other dog, Chelsea, a Chinese Shar-Pei. Missy entered the picture a year before I met her. After having control of the household for six years, Chelsea had begrudgingly accepted Missy.

Generally, the two female dogs got along fairly well, playing together and remaining near their human companion, Sandy. However, Sandy never took the time to train either of them, even though I had been recommended to her by Chow Rescue of Northern Virginia. (Jeryl Ann and Michael McBee, who run the rescue group, insist that all their rescued dogs go through obedience training.)

Sandy contacted me after both dogs had been barking at a passerby, a fight ensued, and Missy took a bite out of Chelsea's stomach. Sandy thought the two dogs would never be able to live together again. When I first met them, Chelsea was still being kept apart from Missy, because the Shar-Pei still had a long healing process ahead.

From the beginning, Missy was cautious around me. She barked at me while hiding behind Sandy. I could see she was fear aggressive. I also noticed that she bossed Sandy around, and when someone passed by the front windows she ferociously attacked and tore at the draperies. Missy needed training. She needed to learn self-confidence and that she did not need to lead her family pack. All of her behaviors pointed at a lack of communication and no sense of where she belonged in her family pack.

While Missy displayed many of the aggressive behaviors mentioned in this chapter (fear, possession, dominance, and redirected aggression), all she really needed was obedience training.

Now the two dogs live together harmoniously, lying at Sandy's feet and walking in tandem down the block without any more outbursts.

Redirected aggression is often mistaken for sibling rivalry. The difference is that sibling rivalry is due to the dogs not knowing their place within the family pack. The dogs haven't received clear direction, in the form of training, from their human companions. Redirected aggression is territorial, not hierarchical. And while the best cure is obedience training, the dog must also learn to redirect his attention in a more positive manner. Reading the calming signals and quickly redirecting the dog are essential for resolving this issue.

Aggression with a Physical Cause

This type of aggression is usually associated with a chemical imbalance, pain from an injury, or other health issues. The dog cannot control when or to whom the aggression is directed. Usually, either there are emotional triggers or a painful area is touched. In other words, there is a reason for the aggressive outburst, but it may be something that is not easily pinpointed.

The best way of approaching this issue is to take the dog to a veterinarian for a complete physical, including a detailed blood analysis. Sometimes a physical cause can be identified, such as epilepsy, thyroid dysfunction, or pain due to injury, a birth defect, or a chronic health condition.

A chronic physical disorder in its early stages may cause behavioral changes that cannot easily be traced to the source, making the dog appear to be aggressive without a reason. But there's always *something* causing the dog to react. Dogs don't just bite without any reason. That would be like you yelling at or trying to strike someone who wasn't there. This can happen to people (and even some animals) with severe psychological conditions such as schizophrenia, but it is not common. A physical source can usually be found.

Dealing with the problem usually includes enlisting the help of a veterinary behaviorist, who can prescribe appropriate drugs to control the cause of the dog's aggression. For example, if the dog has epilepsy, a veterinarian might prescribe phenobarbitol, diazepam (for immediate relief from a severe seizures), or potassium bromide. Thomas Eshbach, DVM, who practices in Fredericksburg, Virginia, prescribes aspirin, Rimadyl, Etogesic, or Duramax for chronic pain from a disease or injury. Sometimes, a combination of medications is needed.

Another possibility is to see a holistic practitioner. Many behavior problems can be solved through holistic means—changing the dog's diet, a new exercise regimen, or adding aromatherapy, flower, or herbal remedies. TTouch (a special form of therapeutic massage developed by Linda Tellington-Jones) helps deal with both pain and stress. Chiropractic manipulation and acupuncture can help relieve pain, giving the dog less reason to react aggressively when touched.

Flower essences that are especially useful for aggressive dogs include aspen, which helps treat fear, anxiety, and apprehension—all of which can lead to fear aggression. Gentian, rockrose, and larch also help with fear aggression, as they aid in building

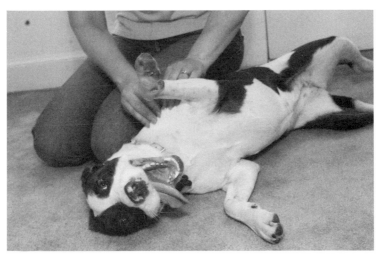

TTouch can be helpful in relieving both pain and stress.

confidence. Oil of bergamot helps balance a dog's emotions. Chamomile relaxes the muscles, aiding in pain relief. Chicory might be helpful to use on a possession aggressive dog. Vine and tiger lily are used on dominant dogs to make them feel less in need of controlling their environment.

Aromatherapy is useful because they quickly penetrate nasal tissue and seep into the surface capillaries, offering direct access to the bloodstream. The essential oils used to create the aromas are produced from an entire plant, offering medicinal qualities that can target illnesses or behavioral issues without the intrusion of forcing the dog to ingest something. The dog simply breathes it in and the response is fairly quick.

Overt Aggression

Overt aggression can be genetic, a learned response, or a complex interplay of the two. Genetically, the dog may have a lower threshold or tolerance and thus more easily triggered into aggressive behavior. For example, dogs who are taught to fight, guard, or attack can lose control of themselves or more easily be triggered into attacking and biting.

You can often recognize this type of aggression because the dog is trying to make himself look larger. The fur along his spine will stand up, his tail will be held up or out stiffly, with ears perked forward, eyes open wide, and body stiff—similar to the dog showing territorial aggression. He'll show all his teeth when (if) he warns, bark loudly as he lunges, and shake his head from side to side as he bites (which is the canine way of making sure the prey is dead).

If you are entering his enclosure, slowly back up and never look him in the eye. If he is coming at you, don't run, because that will trigger his prey drive. Try to turn away and keep your arms folded against your chest. Don't scream or yell. The dog might stop and bark at you, not biting but displaying territorial aggression before an attack. If the owner is close by, calmly tell them to control their dog. All of these reactions are the opposite of what your natural instincts are telling you: Scream and run for your life! But the overtly aggressive dog will run and chase you down, and dogs are faster than people.

In more than three decades as a professional trainer, I have seen only two instances of true overt aggression. One was a Siberian Husky who had been a stray for quite a while before being adopted by a family and totally controlling them. Any attempt at training the dog resulted in a threat to me and to the owner. We never went any further to provoke him into attack, because he was

If a dog is coming at you, stand with your arms folded and turn to the side.

a very large dog and his intentions very clear. The other was a Rottweiler puppy who, at the age of 3 months, showed outright aggressive tendencies, such as attacking his owner without provocation, biting hard enough to break the skin, and not settling down unless he was left alone, locked up without human interaction.

These were unhappy dogs. They were also so aggressive that the only way to deal with them was euthanasia.

While a bite from a fear aggressor might cause bruising or punctures, the attack from an overt aggressor causes far more damage. These dogs mean to injure, not warn. A dog intent on injuring a human or another animal is extremely dangerous. This type of dog has no place in a home environment. Even if one person can control the dog most of the time, that person will not always be present. An overtly aggressive dog is a time bomb, and you have no idea of the time and no way of disconnecting the triggering mechanism.

DEMANDING/DOMINANT AGGRESSION

There is also another type of aggression I have observed over the years. I call it demanding/dominant aggression. It is a kind of dominant aggression and one that is not uncommon in pet dogs—which is why I believe it is worth discussing as a separate issue.

This is a dog who wants something and doesn't get it, but has learned that by making aggressive displays he will get it. He has become the pack leader and rules with an iron jaw. I tend to see this behavior with toy breed dogs who haven't had any training, and in families where the dog had belonged to one of the partners for several years before they got married.

This behavior can be seen in several ways. Perhaps you are sitting and petting the dog and he suddenly growls or snaps. You don't really understand why he suddenly became aggressive. After all, didn't he come to you for attention?

Then there's the dog who lunges and barks at his companions, demanding a play session. When they don't comply, he nips them.

There's also the dog who barks every time his human companions are speaking on the phone or visiting with others.

These are all demanding aggressors. The behavior is very common because it is a learned behavior caused by complacency and inadvertently rewarding the wrong responses.

What happens if you don't pet the dog when he comes to you for attention? He will become more adamant about it by leaning, pushing with his nose, or mouthing your hand. The behavior you reward is the behavior he'll use on his next approach. So if you finally reach down to pet him when he puts his mouth on you, he will start with that behavior next time.

The best way of dealing with demanding aggression is through obedience training and redirection. Once Teddy understands his commands, you can make him perform an appropriate behavior for positive attention instead of demanding your attention through negative behavior. The best example of this is to teach Teddy to sit for attention instead of jumping up or barking for it. Or place him in a down-stay when you are on the phone and reward him for this behavior when you are finished with your phone call.

For a dog who demands playtime, give him more exercise—but how and when you say. Let him play with other dogs, race around the yard, or go for long walks. A dog who is hungry for exercise is more likely to demand attention than one who is tired.

TEMPERAMENT TESTING FOR AGGRESSION

There are several responses your dog can make to stimuli or situations that will let you know how likely it is that he will become aggressive. Teddy's pain threshold is one, social dominance is another, as is his reaction to new objects and situations. The three tests here will help you learn about aggression related to pain, dominant aggression, and fear aggression. These three most common aggressive reactions are the basis for all types of aggression.

Pain Threshold

The lower Teddy's pain threshold, the more likely he is to lash out aggressively, without hesitation, when he is hurting or injured. It's a good idea to know this about your dog, so you can take precautions before treating him for injuries or illness.

The test for this means inflicting minor discomfort, so be sure you are comfortable with the procedures before you start. If you are at all hesitant, speak with your veterinarian, a professional trainer, or a canine behaviorist.

1. Place your dog's paw in your hand.
2. Slide your thumb between his toes and press your thumb into your forefinger, pinching his flesh between.
3. Begin with very light pressure and gradually add pressure until you see some response. You must note both the *length* of time before the response and *how* Teddy responds.

Does he pull his paw away slowly, pull his paw away quickly, yipe as he pulls his paw away, yipe and mouth at you as he pulls his paw away, or bite as he jerks his paw away?

The quicker the response, the lower the pain threshold. The more violent the response, the more likely Teddy will be to react aggressively when he's in pain. For example, a response within two or three seconds, in which Teddy puts his mouth on you as he pulls away, means he might give some warning before biting. Be sure to heed such a warning and try another approach to treatment when he's injured, such as giving him a sedative or a flower remedy before handling him further.

Social Dominance

A dog who is socially dominant ends up running the household, being territorial, and possibly becoming possession aggressive. Knowing that Teddy has this tendency will help you redirect him into a more biddable role in the family pack.

There are two parts to this test: elevating the dog and placing him in a submissive posture.

To elevate him, place your hands behind Teddy's front legs, around his chest, and lift gently until his front feet no longer touch the floor.

If Teddy remains quiet, merely enjoying your touch, he is not displaying any social dominance, because a dominant dog will sometimes feel insecure about being lifted off the floor. If your dog struggles, he might be uncomfortable, but it doesn't necessarily mean he's assertive. If he whines and struggles, he is displaying fear, and he can become fear aggressive. If he puts his mouth on you as he struggles, he is warning you of his displeasure; continuing to hold him up might earn you a bite.

To elevate Teddy, place your hands behind his front legs and lift his front end off the floor.

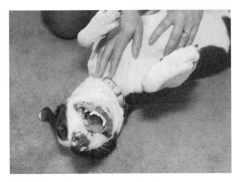

Hold the dog down as he lies on his back.

The second part of the social hierarchy test is to place Teddy into a submissive position, such as rolled over onto his back, holding him down by light pressure on his chest. A submissive dog will lie still and roll his head to the side, while a dominant dog will struggle and try to bite at you. A frightened dog will whine and struggle a bit as well but will not necessarily bite; however, he might be prone to fear aggression in other situations.

Regardless of the response, click only when Teddy is settled and no longer struggling or trying to bite you. Releasing him from this position is a reward, and rewarding him while he is displaying aggression will intensify the response. Wait until he licks, turns his head and eyes, and is no longer stiff. The dog who readily submits will receive his click and reward faster, learning that he produced the appropriate response. The more assertive dog can be shaped into displaying the appropriate response and will gradually decrease his struggling time as he accepts your leadership.

Dogs rarely have to physically hold down a submissive dog; a submitting dog remains in place due to the threat of being bitten. The threat is initiated by showing teeth, snarling, growling, and barking—behavior we cannot possibly emulate. The trick is in the resulting redirection into a positive behavior.

Placing your dog into this submissive position is not always the appropriate way to deal with dominant aggression. It might work in some instances, but heighten his aggression in others.

In this situation, the rollover is only a test to discover the extent of Teddy's dominance tendencies. It is best left to professional dog trainers to apply behavior modification techniques, observe which work best for the individual dog, and then teach you how to apply them.

New Objects and Situations

There are more objects and situations to which Teddy might react than I can write about in one chapter. All you can do is observe your dog when he enters new situations or sees new things. If he is feeling anxious, the first thing he'll do is stop moving. Then he might dip his front end down, circle wide, or bark at the thing that frightens him. If he sees the scary thing move, he might try to flee the area, pulling you behind him.

Once you discover the objects and situations that make Teddy fearful, you can desensitize him the same way you would with any distraction. Build his confidence by taking his mind off the object and refocusing it on receiving rewards for paying attention to you. Soon Teddy will no longer think of the object as scary.

1. Take Teddy to the general vicinity of the scary object.
2. Gradually decrease the distance between him and the scary object through positive associations as you train.
3. Shape his behavior by clicking the moment Teddy looks at you instead of at the scary object.
4. Next, tell him to sit when he looks at you. Click and reward when he does.
5. Increase the duration of the sit by making him wait a few seconds longer each time.

Gradually decrease the distance between your dog and the scary object.

6. Do this in three- to four-foot increments as you decrease the distance between you and the scary object.

7. Repeat as necessary for each scary object or situation.

Confidence is built through obedience. Obedience training also builds knowledge and communication. Communication between you and your dog reduces the need for aggression because you both understand each other.

Now you have a confident, happy, relaxed dog who defers to you instead of taking it upon himself to control his environment and his family pack.

Chapter 9

Clicker Duet

With the increasingly busy lives of most people, the family dog is often left alone for more than eight hours a day, five days a week. But canines are very social creatures and this causes separation issues that can be avoided if the dog has the company of another dog and has also learned to understand his environment through the training process.

At least 30 percent of dog owners have realized that dogs prefer to be in the company of other dogs, as opposed to being left home alone, and consequently have more than one. But people with several dogs sometimes feel daunted in dealing with behavior and obedience routines and often end up giving in to the unwanted behavior of a dog pack. Problems such as rushing doors, destructive chewing, excessive barking and jumping up, pulling on the leash, and overreaction to strangers arise as the dogs feed off one another's anxieties.

Clicker training can change all this. By following the directions in this chapter, you will be able to communicate with as many dogs as you wish at the same time. All will be attentive and eager to respond to your cues. The toughest part will be having each dog perform individually without the others being placed in a stay or in another room. Most dogs are so enthusiastic about clicker training that they want to be the center of the action at all times.

WORKING WITH MORE THAN ONE DOG

There is a definite art to working with more than one dog. This art lies in your timing and use of clear cues. It also relies on the work you do with each dog individually before you begin working them in tandem. While there are some exercises you can teach the dogs to perform together, there are others that require initial one-on-one training.

Dogs love to perform.

To avoid confusion, the dogs need to learn their individual names as well as learning their tandem name. A tandem name is the name you'll use to tell your dogs you are now talking to both or all of them at the same time. (Some examples are Dogs, Guys, Girls, and Puppies.) Using a tandem name will help you get the appropriate response from all parties.

Working with each dog as an individual is an important part of bonding. You want each dog to bond with you as well as with each other. If you only work them in tandem, you'll never achieve this bond.

Because dogs feed off one another's behaviors, you will get the best results doing all initial work in a distraction-free environment. Indoors is best, because it doesn't carry the smells and sounds that trigger the canine prey drive. There is much you can do even in a small space: a short recall, stays, sit, down, stand, and many tricks.

Your dogs will both be eager to work, so they will quickly learn to perform in tandem or they won't reap the rewards. Since you will be working with the clicker to mark the moment, you will need to wait until both dogs have performed the requested task. Otherwise you risk reinforcing the wrong behavior in one of the dogs. This also means the dogs need to learn patience; if one responds before the other, he must recognize that he performed correctly even though his behavior wasn't bridged. This is where praise is helpful. The praise will reinforce the correct response, so the click won't be as necessary to inform Teddy that he did what you requested.

So your tools for tandem work include your vocal and visual cues, the clicker, a pouch filled with treats, your patience and, most important, your imagination. We won't get into using a leash until you must move your training sessions to a distraction-filled environment.

TANDEM TRAINING IN THE BASICS

Before you begin working with both dogs, review the basic commands with each individual dog: come, sit, down, and stay. If you also wish to achieve a tandem stand, practice this individually first. You want to make sure both dogs are quickly responding to all commands before you put them in the distracting situation of working closely together.

You should not have to take more than five to ten minutes to review with each dog. More than that means one dog isn't ready to work in tandem.

If both dogs want to continue but one isn't ready yet, there are two ways you can deal with this. One is to place one of the dogs in a holding area, such as his crate, outside or another room. Another is to place one dog in a down-stay as you work the other. I don't suggest you try this method of separation until both dogs are able to perform their basics in tandem. That's because both dogs will have a heavy drive to respond, and you will have to repeatedly remind the dog who is supposed to be doing a stay that he needs to stay put.

Begin tandem work indoors where there are fewer distractions.

Come

Now that everyone is *warmed up*, let's begin with an easy to learn (and lure) behavior: come. Both Teddy and Freddy

Place one dog in a down-stay while you're working the other.

know this one and will easily respond, but you need to be very quick with their click and reward. If you find it's difficult to do this, you might want to try clicking with your tongue in your cheek instead of using an actual clicker. This leaves both hands free to hold rewards and other tools.

When both dogs arrive, click and reward.

1. Step a short distance away from the dogs and give them the come command.

2. When they arrive, click and reward them both at the same time. (That's why you need both hands free.)

If Freddy lags behind Teddy, praise the dog who arrived but don't click yet. When Freddy gets there, click and reward both. If Freddy doesn't come to you at all, he isn't ready yet to work in tandem. Practice more with him one on one.

Repeat this exercise from ever-increasing distances. You can even play Round Robin (explained in chapter 3) with both dogs at the same time: Go into other rooms or even other floors of the house, if you have them.

Sit-Stay

This exercise can be a little more difficult than come, but if Teddy and Freddy know it well individually, you will see quick success. Always begin with a short period of time without movement or distance. As the dogs perform well together you can then add movement and finally, distance. We break down the behaviors as follows:

1. Give your dogs the cue for sit. Click and reward when both sit down.

2. Give your dogs the cue for sit and then stay.

3. Make them hold that position for no more than ten seconds. Click and reward.

4. Add an additional ten seconds to every subsequent sit-stay until you reach a full minute.

If, at any time, one of the dogs breaks his sit-stay, it means you have breached his behavior threshold. Back up to where both Freddy and Teddy were successfully remaining in their sit-stays. Repeat this level a few times before continuing on to the next level.

You have now come to a point where you need to use each dog's name to differentiate correct behavior from incorrect. Before you started working with both dogs in tandem you had a verbal correction, "no," that you used whenever Teddy didn't respond. You can still use this verbal correction, but now you need to put his name in front of it so he knows you are talking specifically to him: "Teddy, no." The moment the dog is back on track, use his name before the praise: "Teddy, good boy." Because you are doing all this off leash, indoors, there is no way to physically correct or direct the dog. You must rely upon your communication techniques.

When both dogs can remain in a sit-stay for a full minute, begin walking side to side, gradually increasing the criteria to the point where you can walk completely around them. Finally, increase the distance. Take it slow for best success.

Give both dogs the cue for stay.

Down-Stay

The down-stay might be slightly more difficult for Freddy and Teddy to perform in tandem, because one or both might not wish to show submission in the eyes of the other. Lying down means getting into a prone position, and unless your dogs are very comfortable with their place in their hierarchy, there may be issues.

Try to make this exercise as rewarding as possible for both dogs, distracting

Give the dogs little belly rubs to relax them during the down-stay.

them from their instinctive reactions. Give little belly rubs and lots of treats, and begin with very brief down-stays. If there are issues with one dog trying to lie upon any part of the other dog, place them farther apart before giving the down-stay cues. As they get more comfortable, you can gradually bring them closer together.

On-Leash Duo

It's very important for your dogs to be familiar with working in each other's presence before you try on-leash exercises. You will have your hands filled with leashes, clicker, and treats, and therefore won't easily be able to manually help your dogs into their positions.

Walking with you in tandem, the dogs need to be side by side on your left side (if you have taught them to heel on the left). After you've watched Teddy and

Freddy working together, you should have a pretty good idea of who should be closest to you and who can operate a little further away but still keep his attention on you. Let's say Teddy likes to remain very close to you, almost touching you, while responding to your cues. He might be a good candidate for being the *inside* dog. If Freddy doesn't really care about being as close, yet still responds very nicely, he'll make a great *outside* dog. It will be easiest on you if both dogs are consistent in their positions, so make sure they are comfortable.

1. Tell your dogs to perform the sit-stay.

2. Put their leashes on them. Click and reward.

3. Hold the leash of the inside dog in your right hand and the leash of the outside dog in your left hand. Make sure the leash of the outside dog is behind the head of the inside dog.

4. Tell your dogs to heel, using their tandem name before the command.

5. Go forward only five steps, stop, tell them to sit, then click and reward.

6. Gradually increase the number of steps with each successful heel exercise. Mix in sit-stays and down-stays along the way.

Hold the leash of the inside dog in your right hand and the leash of the outside dog in your left hand.

Move forward only five steps on the initial heel command.

Keep the leashes loose enough that they don't constantly pull on your dog's collars, yet tight enough to maintain control when presented with distractions. You don't want your dogs to feel a tug of the leash when they are performing well. Leash pressure is a negative thing to a dog—punishment. Let's try to not inflict this upon dear Teddy and Freddy unless it's absolutely necessary.

Turning is the best way to correct your dogs' positions when they are heeling.

The only way to manually correct the heel of tandem dogs is to turn. If the outside dog starts to move ahead, do a right about turn. If the inside dog begins to move ahead, do a sharp left turn. You might want to use a warning tone, such as "uh-uh," as you turn. This will inform the dogs that you are about to move in a different direction and that they need to direct their attention accordingly. The moment both dogs are back in position, praise, click, and reward. You can also simply praise and continue to the planned stopping point. Praising as the dogs perform encourages them to continue the performance.

Our aim at this point is to teach both dogs to obey simultaneously, regardless of the location of any distractions. We haven't been really strict about their location relative to each other, although having them remain close is how you keep overall control. Now we need to work on each dog's location. We need to get the dogs close enough together so that they work as a team—they move together and stop together.

A coupler helps the dogs teach each other.

The coupler attaches to the dogs' regular collars, not to the training device.

We need to get to the point where a coupler can be attached to their collars without causing distress. A coupler is a connector that has a clip on each side with a ring in the middle for a leash to be attached. The coupler helps with dogs who tend to work unevenly, teaching these dogs how to work closely with each other. Once they are in sync, you can remove the coupler.

Many dogs tend to work better when they're coupled together—especially dogs who are very close, such as siblings who grow up together. I have found that the coupler helps the dogs teach each other. If Freddy is slow to come or heel, Teddy will make him move faster. If Teddy moves too fast, Freddy will slow him down. If Freddy isn't paying attention, Teddy will remind him to respond.

TANDEM TRICK WORK

With both dogs trained to work off leash, they can easily perform many tricks at the same time. I always have my dogs do a couple of tricks before their good-night biscuit or if we're waiting around between takes during a production. It maintains the level of stimulation I need to have them perform in front of the camera. There are many tricks they can perform in tandem: shake, wave, twirl, sit up, speak, jump over or through, roll over, and more.

The only tricks I rarely have them do together are those that involve fetching, because that initiates a kind of competition that I don't want to encourage. There are ways of doing the fetch game in tandem, such as throwing two objects in different directions, but there's always one dog who wants both objects, and that can cause problems.

Shake and Wave

1. Practice the come and sit a few times. Both dogs should be able to follow the same cues as when they worked individually. You still need to have one hand give cues and the other dispense clicks and treats.

Give the shake cue to both dogs as they sit and stay.

2. After cueing the dogs to sit and stay, give the shake cue with your hand.

3. You must wait until both dogs do the shake, then click and reward. You have only one hand to shake both paws, so you will need to have each dog touch the hand before the click. Each dog must wait for his turn to perform.

Often, both dogs will put their paws into your hand at the same time.

At this point you might get one dog waving at you while the other does the shake. This isn't a problem, as long as you don't reward it. Stick to your criteria and click only after both dogs have touched your hand with their paws. As they learn to perform together, both dogs may put their paws in your hand at the same time. It's something they'll often pick up on their own, as this decreases the time between their doing what was cued and receiving the click.

The wave is simply an extension of the shake. Have both dogs sit and stay, then give them the wave cue. The moment they both wave, click and reward. Gradually request longer waves as they learn to perform this trick together.

As the dogs learn to perform the wave, you can up the ante by gradually increasing your distance when you give the cue. As you gain distance, make

Gradually increase your distance on the wave exercise.

sure the cue is away from your body silhouette, because dogs cannot see details at a distance; they only perceive outlines and movement.

Twirl

Here's a new one that you didn't learn in the chapter on tricks. So let's start at the beginning and then transform this into a tandem behavior. Some dogs will instantly learn this trick, while others will require the step-by-step shaping process. We will break it down as follows:

1. Stand and stay. This is the position from which Teddy will perform, so he must be steady on this command.

2. Move the head to one side. As he stands, lure him into moving his head to the side. Click and treat the moment he follows the lure.

3. Move the head and shoulders to one side. Increase the criteria by using the lure to make him move his upper body to the side before the click.

4. Move the upper body a quarter turn. Now his front paws must move along with his upper body. The moment he moves in the right direction, click and treat.

5. Turn the entire body a half circle. Teddy should have the gist of the thing by now, and moving a bit farther won't be hard. Click and reward the moment he has done a half circle. You may want to consolidate at this point and have him perform it a couple of times before moving on.

6. Turn the entire body through three-quarters of a circle. Some dogs don't need to stop at this point; they'll just go all the way around. But if Teddy is at all hesitant, go ahead and click and treat at the three-quarters mark. Teddy is following the lure to make his circle, and this will become your visual cue: your hand twirling around the dog.

7. Turn the entire body totally around in a complete circle. All right, it's a jackpot! Click and give a couple of treats along with petting.

8. Do a complete circle two times, then three times. After doing just one complete circle a couple of times, ask for two and so on until Teddy can do three in a row.

9. Add a verbal command that goes with the visual cue of your hand twirling around the dog.

10. Repeat steps 1 through 9 in the opposite direction. But when it's time to add the verbal cue, use a slight variation such as "twirl" for one way, "other" for the other direction, or simply "left twirl," "right twirl."

Lure Teddy's head to the side.

As Teddy's paws move with his upper body, click and reward.

Do the twirl trick in both directions.

Twirling in tandem is an impressive trick.

To have your dogs perform this in tandem, you will need both hands at first because each dog will be looking for a cue fairly close to his body. When they are adept at the trick, you can use just one hand to cue them both. Of course, both dogs must complete the behavior before the click and reward.

Sit Up

This is another behavior that you start by using both hands to cue the dogs. They have learned to follow the visual cue of your hand pointing upward, and they might initially need a very close hand cue.

Using one hand to cue each dog, give the up command.

1. Begin with both dogs in a sit-stay.

2. Place one hand over the head of each dog with the index finger pointed upward. Say "dogs, up."

3. The moment both dogs are in position, click and treat. Be sure you don't click until both are up, or one of them might get the message that halfway up is just fine.

4. Repeat this a few times using both hands to cue. When the dogs are performing in tandem (that is, both will sit up at the same rate), you can use just one hand to cue them, leaving your other hand free to use the clicker and give treats.

Speak

If you taught your dogs to speak by imitating each other, you've already accomplished this tandem trick. If not, go back to chapter 7 to learn how to teach a dog to speak. Once you have one dog doing this on command, it's very easy to urge the other to do the same. Dogs don't normally allow each other to speak without interrupting.

Jump Over or Through

This is another new trick, and it's loads of fun. Teaching Teddy and Freddy this one will help prepare them for obedience trials, agility, flyball, and more. Regardless of what you have your dog jump over—a pole, high jump, broad jump, water puddle, or hoop—the process is the same.

Let's begin with one dog at a time. When both are adept at going over a hurdle or through a hoop, you can have them perform in tandem.

1. Place a long object on the ground, such as a pole or a board.
2. Heel with Teddy over the object in both directions. As you walk over it, say "over."
3. Click and treat when you have completed each pass.
4. Raise the object a little bit and repeat steps 1 through 3.

Make sure Teddy and Freddy are very comfortable with each level before raising the object a little more. Also make sure *you* can hop over it without falling. Having an accident will totally turn your dog off from wanting to perform this behavior.

Make sure the jump is not so high that you can't get over it with Teddy.

Now it's time to send your dog over the hurdle on his own.

1. Place the dog in a sit-stay on one side of the jump.

2. Go to the other side of the jump, within a couple feet of it, and call your dog by saying "come, over." Scoot backward a bit as he gets near the jump, giving him room to land.

3. Click the moment he jumps over the obstacle.

4. Praise and reward when he arrives.

5. Repeat as you gradually increase the height or width of the jump.

When you're teaching the broad jump, you might need to put the sections on edge to create less of a stepping surface and more height. This will teach your dog to never step on the obstacle but only to jump over it. When he's adept at going over with it spread out a couple of feet, you can lower the longest section in the back, then the middle, and finally the front. Set up this way, your dog can approach the broad jump from one side only: shortest section to tallest. The other jumps can be crossed in both directions.

Place your dog on one side of the jump and have him perform a recall over the jump.

Always have your dog jump over a broad jump from lowest board to the highest.

Whole books have been written about teaching a dog to jump for competitions in obedience, agility, rally-o, and flyball. But here we'll just concentrate on learning a fun trick. So on to tandem jumping.

1. Go back to the heel and jump over the obstacle with the dogs, both individually and then heeling in tandem.

2. Once they are comfortable with this, place both dogs in a sit-stay on one side of the jump and call them with a "come over" command from the other side. You may want to offer a target close to the jump. The target can be a stick or your hand.

3. As they come toward you, back up a bit.

4. Click as they go over the jump. Reward when they arrive in front of you.

You want your dogs to learn the entire behavior chain of sit-stay, come, and jump over, so you will need to gradually work toward clicking only when the behavior chain is complete. For example, you first will click when they jump. When they fully understand this, you click when they have already jumped and are coming to you. Finally, you click when they have arrived in front of you.

If you find that one or both dogs are going around the jump instead of over it, you'll need to back up a bit. Return to working them individually. Teddy and

Have both dogs perform a recall over the jump.

Heel both dogs over the jump.

Freddy must both be comfortable and reliable as individuals before you attempt the trick in tandem. Remember, working the dogs in tandem automatically sets up a distraction. Both dogs must be reliable and fully understand everything you want from them before you can ask either to perform in such a distracting environment.

Tandem Hoop Jump

To jump through a hoop, you'll need to use your target stick. Again, begin by teaching this skill to one dog at a time. The fastest way to do that is to lure the dog through from one side of the hoop to the other with the hoop resting on the floor. This way, Teddy can first learn that he's supposed to move through something instead of over it.

When he is comfortable with moving through, you can raise the hoop off the floor a little bit. Use a visual and verbal cue that is distinctly different from jumping over. I usually say "go through" as I swing my arm, holding the target stick, from one side to the other. The arm I use depends on which direction the dog is moving from point A to point B. If Teddy is going from left to right, I use my right arm; from right to left, I use my left arm. The other arm is holding the hoop.

By now Teddy and Freddy should be very adept at following cues, so it should be fairly easy for them to transfer from jumping over to jumping through, once they understand the shape of the object you wish them to move through.

1. Place both dogs in a sit-stay.
2. Hold the hoop two to four feet in front of them, with the bottom resting on the floor.

3. Give the "go through" cues.

4. Once both dogs have jumped through, click and reward.

5. Gradually increase the height of the hoop from the floor until you reach your goal.

I normally don't make my dogs jump through in tandem with the hoop more than two feet off the floor. However, it would be easy enough to shape the behavior to have them jump higher, since they already understand the basic concept.

Use the target stick to help guide the dogs through the hoop. They'll need to go through one at a time.

Roll Over

This tandem trick requires great timing and a pair of dogs who don't mind touching each other while they are lying down. If Teddy and Freddy have any personal space issues while they are in a down-stay, do not attempt this trick, as it may cause a little spat if one accidentally rolls onto the other. If both dogs are relaxed and paying attention to you, though, this trick shouldn't be too difficult.

1. Place both dogs in down-stays, side by side, facing the same direction.

2. They both should already know how to roll over. You will need to use both hands—one to cue each dog—as you give the visual cue and verbal command.

3. If you are asking them to roll to your left, give the dog on that side the cue first.

4. As the first dog is beginning his rollover, cue the second dog.

5. When both dogs complete the exercise, click and treat both of them.

As Teddy and Freddy become comfortable with and adept at this trick, you can add more than one roll. They can do it twice, three times, or more. Using slightly

---

I once watched an act on *Late Night with David Letterman* where two Border Collies performed to very subtle cues from their trainer. He merely moved his head or made a slight motion of his hand. The two dogs performed many tricks in perfect tandem. One was to roll over in each direction. It was like watching a pair of dancers.

Begin the rollover with both dogs lying side by side.

First cue one dog, then the other.

different cues, they can also learn to roll in both directions. Again, teach them this skill individually before trying it in tandem, because dogs tend to have favorite sides, just as we do. What might be easy on one side isn't as easy on the other. And if you want them to perform together, they must be equally comfortable on both sides.

TANDEM TRAINING IN THE DISTRACTION ZONE

Whenever you add distractions, you are adding an entirely new dimension to the training process. This is especially true when you're working with more than one dog, because they tend to feed off each other's behavior, causing even bigger reactions.

Desensitizing a group of dogs to the presentation of distractions is done the same way as you did when you were working each individual dog. Begin with the distraction at a far enough distance that it does not cause a reaction. Gradually work closer and closer until Teddy and Freddy don't care about anything except paying attention to you.

Now you can take off both the coupler and the leashes.

Before taking your dogs out in public in tandem, be very aware of their distraction weaknesses. If you are likely to run into those distractions while working your dogs, make sure Teddy and Freddy have first learned good self-control. If one dog reacts, you can be sure the other will.

I remember one particular example of a multiple dog feeding frenzy among three Boston Terriers. One was a female, Cleo, and the other two were males, Ptoly and Antony. Alone they performed very well, even in the presence of other dogs. Their owner and I had them working off leash on everything, even in a group—all three. The main problems occurred when Cleo and Ptoly, in particular, passed another dog. One would bark at the dog and then the other would lunge at him. Soon, both were barking and lunging at the other dog. Antony would then join in, and all three Bostons were going at it. It took a lot of distraction-proofing during group training sessions to overcome this problem.

Being aware of the triggers and the way the dog behaves just before a reaction will help you head off the problem. If you see either dog displaying a prereaction behavior, quickly redirect him, perhaps by turning and changing your pace. It would be a good idea, then, to go back to working the dogs individually in the presence of the distraction for a while before working in tandem again.

There will be times when you can't avoid a distraction. If your dogs are still easily triggered into a reaction, they should wear a training device appropriate for their temperaments: a Sense-sation harness for the light pullers and a head halter for the heavy pullers. When using the head halter or Sense-sation harnesses, attach the coupler to your dogs' regular neck collars so you don't interfere with the action of their training devices.

If you're using a Sense-sation harness while working the dogs, be sure to keep both leashes fairly taut so that you can quickly use them when needed. If you're using a head halter, keep some slack in the leashes because you don't want to put

Distraction-proofing with two dogs can be difficult, because they react to each other's emotions.

Working several dogs with head halters makes distraction-proofing easier.

any pressure on Teddy's and Freddy's noses unless they are being redirected. If only one dog requires this guidance, apply the pressure only to that particular dog, not to both. This is the reason you should work with individual leashes before using just one, or none. One dog may have everything down pat, while the other is a clown or tends to be easily distracted. But a dog who is performing well yet is receiving corrections will quickly sour to the experience.

Using a clicker while working two dogs on two different leashes may prove difficult for many. You may want to switch to a click sound in your cheek, or simply praise when Teddy and Freddy are good. When you can work with them off leash in tandem, you'll have a hand available again to use your clicker.

More Than Two

If you have more than two dogs, I suggest you begin by working only two at a time. When all of them can perform off leash with reliability in the distraction zone, you can work all of them simultaneously. While it might be difficult for them to heel side by side, it won't be a problem for them to perform stays in any position and recalls from any location.

Just as when you were working with only two dogs, the click happens when all of the dogs have completed the task. Some of them may need to acquire a bit of patience, while the others learn to speed up their responses. These skills can be taught individually before working the dogs in a group.

Chapter 10

Clicking Unlimited

Now that Teddy knows all of his obedience commands both on and off a leash, it's time to consider what you're going to do with all that talent! Your dog is great to be around, listens well at home, is fun to take with you on outings, and travels well. You are very proud of Teddy and want the world to know all about his accomplishments.

Long books have been written about the intricacies of each type of competition I will discuss here, so this chapter will just give you an overview of the many ways you can use clicker training to help you show off your beloved canine companion's beauty, brains, and talent. You and Teddy are a team. Together, you can go anywhere and do anything you set your sights on. With clicker training, you can shape any behavior and be sure to have fun in the process.

CONFORMATION

Conformation shows are for purebred dogs. Each dog is judged on structure, coat, movement, and overall appearance, and is compared against a written standard of perfection for the breed. The winning dog of each breed is the one who most closely exemplifies the standard for his breed. Each breed winner is then judged in comparison to the other breed winners in his group, and finally, the group winners are judged against other breed group winners for Best in Show.

Serious breeders use conformation shows to discern top-quality breeding dogs. Westminster Dog Show and Crufts Dog Show are two of the world's largest breed shows, displaying dogs who have earned championships and high points throughout the year at other dog shows. Winning the breed honors at a national show is a huge accomplishment.

There are three behaviors a dog must perform with pizzazz in the show ring: gaiting, stacking, and stand-for-examination. In gaiting, the dog must strut a little in front of his handler, body held in a happy, proud manner, showing off how well he moves. When stacking, the dog must stand perfectly still, ears, body, legs, and tail in the appropriate position for his breed. All dogs are physically examined by the judge. From the tips of their noses to teeth, head, neck, shoulders, hips, legs and tail, the judge will touch all of these parts to properly assess the dog's body structure.

The dogs who win their breed, group, and Best in Show honors have exquisite structure and coats, good temperament, and show well. A dog will only show well if he is enjoying himself. Few dogs will show to the best of their abilities if they are frightened, cowed by their handler, or don't wish to be there.

While some dogs will give their all for a toy or food treats, others will be so overwhelmed by the noise and activity of the show, or the shared tension of their handler, that they'd rather stay in their comfortable crates than strut around a ring.

It isn't easy to be a good handler in this sport. It takes years of practice and the mentoring of other handlers. Many of the professional handlers had their start as junior handlers or assistants to the pros, learning their craft and perfecting their ability to show their dogs in the best possible light.

However, while they understand the goals of earning points and championships, the dogs do not. All they know is whether they receive praise or punishment for the things they do. While some are easily rewarded by the presence of a cheering crowd, others are frightened by this commotion. While some dogs care more about the squeaky toy in their handler's hand than the fact that a stranger is touching them all over, other dogs want to run and hide.

Clicker training can help those dogs who are insecure or fearful adapt better to the show life. It can also help them attain a better show attitude, teaching them how to hold their bodies and strut their stuff with more confidence.

A good performance in the conformation ring catches the judge's eye.

Gaiting

The art of gaiting the dog to his best advantage is important in a conformation show. The dog must move with grace and look like he's having a great time. This can be achieved through shaping.

1. Using a regular lightweight collar, run forward with your dog.

2. When he's running alongside you happily, click and reward.

3. Repeat this until Teddy is instantly striking up a happy prance. Add a distinct visual cue for the behavior and mark the moment your dog performs his gaiting on cue.

4. Gradually reduce your other visual cue of running as you reward Teddy for his continued strut.

If Teddy gets too far ahead of you, turn around and reward him the instant he's with you again, strutting proudly.

What can be more fun than running along with you and being rewarded for it?

Stacking

Each breed has its own stacking style, intended to show off the special characteristics of the breed, but in general the judge would like to see tails held proudly, shoulders and hips square or stretched, legs straight, head and ears up and forward. Regardless of the stacking style in your breed, you can get your dog to stand the way you'd like him to using clicker training and behavior shaping techniques.

Break the exercise down into small components as follows:

Stand and stay.

Stand and stay with head held proudly.

Stand and stay with head and ears in the correct positions.

Stand and stay with head, ears, and tail in the correct positions.

These components can be further broken down into smaller goals, if need be. Always begin with a small goal and build on it to accomplish the big picture.

Suppose you have a dog who doesn't like to stand still and won't hold his head, ears, or tail in the correct position. You'd begin by teaching him to stand and stay in the correct manner.

1. Lure Teddy into a stand. Click and reward.

2. Make him remain in that stand a moment longer. Click and reward.

3. Gradually increase the amount of time Teddy must stand still before he earns his click. When he can remain in place for more than a minute, you can begin working on the other aspects of his stacking exercise.

There is a stacking style for every breed.

Let's go to the head next.

1. Make a noise, such as a squeak, cluck, or kissing sound. The moment he alerts to the sound by looking at you, click and reward.

2. Repeat a couple times until Teddy begins to anticipate the sound by looking alert. Click and reward.

3. Now you need to teach him to hold his head correctly. He shouldn't be looking at you. For this, use your target stick or target hand. Have Teddy target with his nose in the correct direction and position. Click and reward the moment he does so.

4. Gradually shape him to hold that position for longer and longer periods of time.

A proper stack shows off the dog's best attributes.

Finally, we'll do the tail. Teddy has learned to stand still while holding his head and ears forward, so you must do something to get him a little excited. The squeaky noise, for example, might cause him to lift his tail. Or a high, happy tone of voice used in praise. The moment his tail is near the position you want, click and reward. Gradually shape Teddy to the point where he will hold his tail in the proper place along with the other positions needed for stacking.

Granted, with many dogs it may not be this easy. You might have to break each small goal into even smaller goals, because stacking has many nuances that require a more intuitive understanding of how and when to stand the dog in just the right way. You may need to work with a professional handler and be dedicated to years of showing before you attain the perfect stack for your breed.

Stand for Examination

This is an exercise that should be taught to all dogs, whether you are showing your dog or not. It just makes sense for a dog to learn to remain still while being he is examined, since he will

A dog in a conformation show must stand still while being examined by the judge.

receive veterinary care, grooming, and health checks regularly throughout his life. Teddy must be amenable to such handling for his own well-being.

In chapter 3, I explained how to teach Teddy to stand and stay. To carry these behaviors over to the conformation ring, you need to take your dog to these events and ask everyone you can to touch your dog as you click and reward him for standing still. This will make the entire process a positive experience for Teddy. He'll soon learn to associate the events with meeting a lot of people who dispense treats. Each stranger will be like going up to another vending machine that holds treats, only Teddy doesn't have to push any buttons. He merely has to stand still while they stroke his coat, which is another rewarding experience for him.

OBEDIENCE

Obedience trials are held in three levels: Novice, Open, and Utility. Each level has its own classes and challenges. Competitors also accumulate points toward the titles of Utility Dog Excellent (UDX) and Obedience Trial Champion (OTCh).

To earn an obedience title, a dog must compete in enough shows to earn three "legs" under three different judges. Each leg earned means the dog has scored a minimum of 170 out of 200 possible points. The amount of time this takes doesn't matter. A dog can earn a title in a week or seven years. The legs never expire.

Novice Classes

The title for this level is called Companion Dog (CD), because the exercises required to earn this title are those that every companion dog should know.

Granted, companion dogs don't have to perform as precisely as one does in an obedience trial, but the general behaviors are the same. The Novice group is divided into Novice A and Novice B. The first class is for handlers who have never before put a CD title on any dog. Novice B is for handlers who *have* taken a dog to the CD level. Judges often make the obedience routines in Novice B a little more challenging than those in Novice A, because the handlers tend to be more experienced, with dogs who are well prepared.

There are individual exercises and group exercises in each class.

In the individual exercises, you and Teddy enter the ring without any other dogs or handlers. It's just you, Teddy, and the judge. The judge tells you what to do, sort of like playing Simon Says. The first exercise is usually on-leash heeling. You will be told to go forward, turn left, turn right, about turn (a 180-degree turn, always to the right), move slow, or move fast. Your normal gait should be a brisk walk to ensure that the fast and slow paces look very different. You will be asked to stop two to four times. The pattern is solely up to the judge.

The next exercise is a figure-8 around two posts (show stewards usually play the role of "post"). The judge will direct the handler-dog team to go forward and halt in this figure two to three times.

Following this is the stand for examination. Remember that one? It's a very important aspect of obedience trials, too. The dog is placed in a standing position

The figure-8 exercise in the Novice class. The show stewards are the "posts."

with the handler standing in front of him, six feet away. The judge approaches the dog, touches his head, shoulders, and hips, then moves off, telling the handler to return to position. The dog is not supposed to move his feet at all. He can watch his handler, wag his tail, pant, or grin, but cannot move until the judge signals that the exercise is complete.

The next exercise is heeling off the leash. The pattern is usually the same as, or similar to, the one done on leash. This tests the dog's reliability without a tether between him and his handler. Of course, a dog can only heel well on leash if the leash really isn't needed anyway. So off-leash work shouldn't be any more difficult.

The final individual exercises are the recall and finish. The handler places the dog in a stay in the heel position. The judge directs the handler to leave the dog, and the handler then signals the dog to stay, walks directly in front for thirty feet, turns, and faces the dog. The judge then tells the handler to call the dog. The dog must come directly in front of the handler and sit automatically. The dog's pace should be brisk. No sniffing, weaving, or visiting with other exhibitors along the way. No chasing after the equipment in adjacent arenas, either. (This can prove quite amusing to the spectators, but not to the dog's handler.) Once the dog arrives and sits, the judge directs the handler to finish. This means the dog should place himself into the heel position by going around the handler either to the left or the right.

There's quite a bit more to all this than I've described in these paragraphs. Entire books are devoted to each nuance of obedience trials, from how to teach a dog to perform to learning how to handle the dog in the ring. The handler and dog are a team, and each must do their part to perform with precision in order to achieve high scores.

The group exercises are long stays: a one-minute sit-stay and a three-minute down-stay. There are up to twelve dogs lined up side by side, two feet apart, in heel position with their handlers. When the judge signals to leave the dogs, the handlers tell their dogs to stay, walk thirty feet in front of them, turn, and face their dogs. The handlers remain in place until the judge tells them to return to their dogs. The dogs must remain in either the sit or the down position (depending on which exercise you are doing at the time) until the handlers return to heel position and the judge signals that the exercise is complete. If any dog moves out of position, he will be disqualified from the class, meaning he has no chance of earning a leg toward his CD title at this trial.

When all the competitors in the class have completed the individual and group exercises, the scores are tallied up. Points are taken away for sloppy heeling, poor sits, sniffing, being distracted, visiting with the judge or stewards, forging ahead, lagging behind, and a host of other faults. It is up to the judge how severely each fault is scored.

If you have worked with Teddy on all the exercises in this book, you should be ready to show the world how well your dog can perform. Why not give this a try?

Group stay exercises are tough for some dogs, but not this group.

Before any competition, it's a good idea to take Teddy to a few shows and walk around, giving him a chance to get used to the ambiance and stress of an obedience trial. There are more distractions at a show than I can list, and there's no way of preparing for them elsewhere.

Because sanctioned shows (shows where points are accumulated and titles are awarded) don't allow animals on the grounds who aren't entered in the show, you should attend matches. These are practice trials for those who need to learn what their weaknesses are and also a chance to acclimate the dog to the show environment. Matches also offer a class called Sub-Novice for dogs who are still unreliable off leash among the show distractions. In Sub-Novice, all exercises are done on leash. Sometimes it's the handler who needs the extra assurance, not the dog. This is a great way to gain confidence in yourself.

You cannot use the clicker in the obedience ring during competition. But you can use it to teach Teddy exactly what you want him to do. To achieve high scores, you can shape his behavior as follows:

1. Make sure Teddy understands all the commands he needs to know for the Novice classes: heel, sit-stay, down-stay, recall, finish, and stand-stay.

2. As Teddy performs each exercise with more precision, click and reward him. Do not click if he offers sloppy responses—for example, he sits but doesn't sit squarely in the appropriate position at your left leg, facing forward. You can attain this precision by gradually shaping the position. Each time he does it better than the last time, click and reward. Allow this level of response up to three times, then require the next level of precision before marking his success.

3. Ask Teddy to perform more than one exercise correctly before clicking, until he can perform all of the individual exercises before he gets his click. Add on exercises gradually, because you don't want your dog to lose interest. If he loses interest at any point, back up to the place in the routine where he was still paying attention and work at this level for a while. When he is once again proficient, add another exercise before the click.

4. Gradually replace the sound of the clicker with prompt praise. You cannot use a clicker in the ring but you can praise Teddy between exercises, which will let him know he is performing well and will get his reward when he's done. When you leave the ring, you can give him loads of praise, petting, toys, and treats.

Open Classes

This level is very challenging for many dogs as well as for their handlers. It can be a big jump, literally, because the exercises involve reasoning, fast response, and athletic ability. The Open exercises include off-leash heeling, off-leash figure-8s around two stewards, a drop on recall, retrieving both on a flat surface and over a high jump, and jumping over a broad jump. The jump height and width depend on the dog's size.

The group exercises are similar to those in Novice, only the stay times are longer and the handlers are out of sight. The sit-stay is three minutes and the down-stay is five minutes. But when you're waiting out of sight and wondering if your dog is staying, it can seem like three to five hours instead.

All of the exercises for the Open level have been discussed in previous chapters. Off-leash obedience is a necessity for every dog regardless of where or how he lives, because without this skill the dog's ability to exercise and socialize is very limited.

Retrieving over a jump can be a challenging exercise.

The drop-on-recall (the dog must stop and lie down instantly at any point while he is coming to you) is important when calling your dog from a long distance, because something might be on a collision course with your dog—for example, you are calling your dog from across a street and see a vehicle coming. Being able to have him drop to the ground until the obstacle passes can be a lifesaver.

Having a dog who can retrieve is a great way of interacting with Teddy. It's relaxing for you, entertaining for him, and there are endless variations on this activity. Jumping over something along the way is one of them. Many dogs love to jump anyway, and directed jumping can be loads of fun.

So, as you can see, knowing all the exercises in Open just gives you and Teddy more to do together. You don't have to compete to enjoy the benefits of training these skills.

Utility Classes

This level of obedience is very difficult to attain. Exhibiting in Utility requires a lot of dedication, a high energy level, and a dog who can concentrate for long periods of time. Herding and sporting breeds tend to offer the best overall performances at this level, but dogs in other breeds have also done well.

The exercises include an off-leash heeling pattern done only with visual cues. Another exercise is the stand for examination, in which the handler leaves the dog and walks more than twenty feet away. After the judge touches the dog, the handler must call the dog to heeling position. This exercise alone requires steadfastness, trust, and a quick response to subtle visual cues.

The next exercise is called the directed retrieve. Three identical, numbered gloves are laid out across the ring behind the handler. The judge tells the handler which glove is to be retrieved. The handler and the dog turn as the handler tells the dog which glove to retrieve. As Teddy is sent to retrieve a glove, the handler gives a specific direction cue, such as leaning down a little, bending the arm at the elbow, or pointing his fingers at the glove Teddy must fetch.

You start by teaching Teddy to fetch one glove. When he is adept at that, two are placed and a number is added to the verbal cue: "fetch one" or "fetch two." The visual cue is the same, and since Teddy has already learned to respond to this visual cue, the verbal cue will quickly be learned as he is reinforced for responding in the

---

I once saw a Sheltie and her owner perform a great scent discrimination exercise. Her owner put a pile of coins on a blanket and directed her dog to choose a specific quarter from the pile. The dog performed the task perfectly on every try. I had never before seen such a great exhibition of scent discrimination work. Kudos to the two of them for all their hard work and their desire to reach higher goals. It was an amazing exhibition!

appropriate way. Once he understands the exercise with two gloves, you can add a third. To make it easier, you might want to begin with the gloves a good distance apart. This will make it less likely for Teddy to fetch the wrong glove. Remember that you want to build on success not failure, so set Teddy up for success. Once he can perform a directed retrieve for all three gloves and understands the verbal cue number sys-

Scent discrimination requires the dog to use his natural abilities.

tem, you can move the gloves closer together. You can be assured, however, that they will rarely be closer than ten feet apart in the show ring. It would be a good idea to practice with them a little closer, though, because you never know when a show steward might challenge your dog just a little more by dropping the gloves closer together.

The directed retrieve is followed by the scent discrimination exercise. There are ten identical articles—usually single-, double-, or triple-bar dumbbells made of metal or leather. All are laid out on the ground at least ten feet behind the handler and dog. The handler touches only one. The judge then takes this article and places it with the others. The judge tells the handler to send the dog, and the handler and the dog then turn, and the dog must retrieve the article with the handler's scent. This exercise is done once with a metal article and once with a leather article.

The scent discrimination exercise can be taught just the way you taught Teddy games with different toys. You will simply direct his retrieve using your scent, rather than shape, as the differentiating factor. Begin by having Teddy retrieve an obedience dumbbell article with your scent (a game he already knows, since anything you touch has your scent on it). When he is reliable, try it with two identical articles: one with your scent, one without. (Each article should have a number on it so you can remember which is which.) Direct Teddy to retrieve the article with your scent. Click and reward only when he retrieves the one you wanted. If he returns with the other one, give him the *keep going* signal. He'll soon return with the one you wanted, upon which you click and reward. As he becomes adept at discerning between two articles, go to three and keep building.

Then switch to the other article material. If you were using a metal article for the first practice exercises, use a leather article next, and begin again. As Teddy is learning this exercise, his brain will also be developing a higher form of reasoning ability.

As if this weren't challenging enough, the next two exercises are the go out and directed jumping. For a dog trained using the procedures outlined in this book, this really won't seem very difficult, especially after he has already learned the previous exercises. Your dog already knows how to target. A go out is merely moving to and touching a target, with the added request of the dog turning and sitting once he touches it. You can easily shape the behavior as follows:

1. Gradually increase the distance of the target with each successful touch.

2. Once Teddy is good at going to touch the target, tell him to sit after he touches it. Click and reward the moment he does so.

3. When he learns the pattern of touch and sit, click only after he sits when turning to look at you.

4. The final step is to click only when he sits facing you.

The directed jump is similar to having Teddy wave with either his right or left paw. He already knows the trick; you just need to change the cues a little to add a recall. You have already taught Teddy all of the behaviors associated with this exercise, so you don't need any backchaining in the training procedures.

1. Begin this exercise by teaching Teddy direction cues using your outstretched arms, because this body language is easily identifiable from a distance. Teach Teddy to go touch targets both on your left and right, using your arms to cue the direction.

2. Next, add a board or pole on the ground that Teddy will have to cross over to reach his target. Make sure to do this in both directions. By this point Teddy should have a good idea of what your direction cue means.

3. Add a small jump where the poles were. Now you should also add the voice command for jumping as you give the direction visual cue. For example, you can say "over left" or "over right" as you lift your arm to shoulder height on each side, respectively.

4. Next, add the recall cue. If Teddy is uncertain about coming to you after targeting, you can begin by practicing this part without the rest of the exercise; however, this is assuming that you and Teddy are beyond recall issues and can easily add a recall to the over left or over right cues.

RALLY-O

Rally-o is a relatively new canine sport that emphasizes the enthusiasm and teamwork of the dog and handler. They must perform a series of exercises similar to those in competitive obedience, only quickness and attitude count more than precision. The higher scores are for those teams that move smoothly through the course, completing each exercise with accuracy and with the fewest cues.

Two organizations offer rally-o titles: the American Kennel Club (AKC) offers titles only to purebred dogs, and the Association of Pet Dog Trainers (APDT) offers titles to all dogs.

In a rally-o course, each station has instructions for tasks you and your dog must perform.

AKC competitions have two levels. In Level 1, the classes are done all on a leash and include twelve to fifteen stations or numbered locations, where a posted sign signals the exercise to be performed. The Level 2 classes are done off leash and have twelve to eighteen stations, including at least one jump.

The entire course is done in the heel position. The stations consist of heeling at different paces, turns in both directions, circles, halts, spirals, and sending the dog over jumps. Some other exercises are the finish to the left while taking a step forward; the 1-2-3 halt, in which the handler takes one step forward, halts, then two steps, halts, and finally, three steps and halts; and one of the more challenging movements, in which the dog must move into heel position while the handler moves straight sideways to the left or right.

You can find the list of exercises on the rally-o web site at www.rallyobedience.com, or directly on the AKC web site at www.akc.org.

All of the exercises in rally-o are either the same as what you and Teddy are already performing, or simple variations, making it fun and easy to participate in this sport.

CANINE FREESTYLE

Canine freestyle is a dog and handler routine set to music and one's own imagination. Essentially, it's a choreographed set of exercises that involves various heeling positions, turns, pivots, side and diagonal passes, pace changes, and tricks. Other optional movements include weaving, rolling over, crawling, jumping, and spinning. I've even seen performances where two or more dogs danced with their handler, and team performances where several handler-dog couples interacted with another handler-dog couple.

Several organizations offer titles in this sport for dogs of either purebred or mixed heritage. The titles are separated into levels with ever-increasing routine times and required elements.

The Canine Freestyle Organization has four competition levels. In Level 1 the handler and dog do all the movements on leash within one and a half to two and a half minutes. They are required to do heel work on either the left or right side, pace changes and circles, and serpentines or spirals. In Level 2 all these things must be done off leash within the same period of time, plus the heel work must be done on both sides. Level 3 requires more complex combinations of movements with a greater emphasis on how the performance is choreographed. All the exercises are done off leash within two to three minutes. The dog must perform heeling patterns from both sides, pace changes, turns or pivots, circles or serpentines or spirals, back up, and show some lateral work, such as moving left or right.

Level 4 is based upon an artistic presentation of the fully trained canine athlete. The performance at this level is two and a half to nearly four minutes long and requires heel work from both sides, three pace changes, turns and pivots, circles, serpentines or spirals, backing up, lateral work, and distance work. Add-ons such as jumps and other tricks add to the score.

With Teddy's knowledge of obedience, tricks, and overall distraction proofing, competing in canine freestyle is limited only by your ability to choreograph all of his skills into a routine. With practice, Teddy will learn the pattern and enjoy moving to the music with you.

Shaping the routine can be as basic as teaching any of the complex behaviors you've already accomplished. Begin with two or three skills and build from there. Always observe your dog for signs of boredom or fatigue and allow frequent rest periods. Challenge yourselves and you'll both achieve *beyond* basic training.

AGILITY

Agility was born in 1977 at the Crufts Dog Show in England. Britain is famous for its horse show jumping competitions, and the organizers of the Crufts Dog Show thought it might be fun to do the same with dogs. Although it started as an exhibition, it proved so popular that agility became a competitive sport. It's high-energy fun for both the spectators and the dog-handler teams. Since its debut in the United States in 1986, agility has become an international canine sport. It is widely televised and enjoyed around the world.

Many agility organizations offer titles. The AKC titles are for purebreds only, but the United States Dog Agility Association, the North American Dog Agility Council, and the Agility Association of Canada, among many others, offer titles for all dogs.

All of the obstacles used in agility are easily taught using clicker training methods. The dogs have a great time, so the activity eventually becomes self-rewarding.

Training your dog to handle all the obstacles on an agility course will take some time, but you'll both have a lot of fun.

The course is run off leash to prevent any collars being caught on obstacles, so your dog must be very reliable with a myriad of distractions around.

Some of the obstacles negotiated in an agility course include:

- Contact obstacles. These include a seesaw, dogwalk, A-frame, and various ramps. The dog must touch a specific zone (normally a yellow area) both ascending and descending, and remain on the obstacle for its entire length.

- Pause table. This is raised platform on which the dog must do a down-stay for at least five seconds.

- Weave poles. There are twelve poles set in a straight row, and the dog must weave in and out of them. He may not miss a single pole during his weave.

- Tunnels. There is an open tunnel that is curved so the dog cannot see the exit as he enters, and a collapsed fabric tunnel in which the dog enters the open part and must move through the collapsed end to exit.

- Jumps and hurdles. There are a variety of these, including a solid high jump, tire jump, bar jumps, double bar jumps, broad jumps, and even the spreads and parallel jumps often seen in horse jumping competitions.

The dog is timed, and time penalties are added for faults such as missing an obstacle or running them in the wrong order. No food or toy rewards are allowed on the course, but you do run with the dog and can give visual and verbal cues.

While it might be fun to train Teddy for agility, you should also consider training yourself, because it requires athleticism on your part as well. You'll have to be able to sprint, turn, direct Teddy, and do all this while keeping the order of the obstacles in your head. The handlers are allowed to study the course before working their dogs through it, but the excitement of the moment can challenge anyone's memory.

Even if you don't wish to actually compete in an agility trial, it's loads of fun for you and Teddy to learn how to work the obstacles and do run-throughs now and then.

OTHER FUN ACTIVITIES

There are a limitless number of other fun canine activities, such as K9 flying disc, hunting and field trials, flyball, tracking, schutzhund, lure coursing, weight pulling, herding, mushing, earthdog, terrier races, scent hurdles, and carting. The Internet is filled with information about these sports, and there are multitudes of articles and books written about them, as well. A little research may open your eyes to a totally new activity for you and your dog.

You and Teddy are now able to communicate with each other through vocal tones and visual cues, so it's Clicking Unlimited! There is no limit to the behaviors you can teach your dog. Just approach each new activity with a positive attitude and be ready to reward your dog for each success—big or small.

Appendix

Internet Resources

Here are some useful resources for finding clicker training supplies, books, articles, and trainers.

www.miriamfields.com
Miriam Fields-Babineau (the author of this book) has a web site featuring articles, training information, and links to supplies. She also sells training supplies she has designed, including The Comfort Trainer and All-in-One Leash, and many of her books.

www.akc.org
The American Kennel Club web site includes articles, event schedules, and information about AKC breeds.

www.anxietywrap.com
Susan Sharp's web site featuring articles; she also developed and sells the Anxiety Wrap, a kind of jacket for dogs and cats that uses all-over light pressure to ease anxiety.

www.apdt.com
The Association of Pet Dog Trainers web site has articles, event schedules, a recommended list of books and videos, and an international list of member dog trainers.

www.cleanrun.com
The web site of Clean Run, a magazine about agility competition, features articles, training supplies, and gifts.

www.clickandtreat.com
Clicker trainer Gary Wilkes's web site features articles, event schedules, books, and training supplies.

www.theclickercompany.com
The Clicker Company web site sells training supplies.

www.clickersolutions.com
Melissa Alexander's web site featuring articles, books, web links, and a trainer list.

www.clickertrain.com
The Clicker Train web site features articles and training supplies.

www.clickertraining.com
Clicker guru Karen Pryor's web site features articles, event schedules, books, training supplies, and a list of trainers.

www.dogpatch.org
The Dog Patch web site features articles and training supplies.

www.dogpro.org
The International Association of Canine Professionals web site features articles, event schedules, and a list of member dog trainers.

www.dogwise.com
Dog Wise is an online bookstore specializing in pet books and dog training supplies.

www.jjdog.com
J and J Dog Supplies offers training supplies, books, and videos.

www.pet-shop.net
The Little River Pet Shop web site offers training supplies.

www.puppyworks.com
Puppy Works sponsors educational dog events for dog trainers, behaviorists, breeders, veterinarians, and dog enthusiasts. The web site features articles and event schedules for seminars.

www.uwsp.edu/psych/dog/obed.html
Dr. P's Dog Training web site features articles and numerous links to other sites for more articles, supplies, and trainers.

Index